WHY WE SHOULD CALL OURSELVES CHRISTIANS

WHY WE SHOULD CALL OURSELVES CHRISTIANS

THE RELIGIOUS ROOTS OF FREE SOCIETIES

Marcello Pera

Translated by L.B. Lappin

ENCOUNTER BOOKS · NEW YORK · LONDON

First American edition published in 2011 by Encounter Books,
an activity of Encounter for Culture and Education, Inc.,
a nonprofit, tax exempt corporation.
Encounter Books website address: www.encounterbooks.com

Originally published in Italy as *Perché Dobbiamo Dirci Cristiani* in
2008 by Arnoldo Mondadori Editore S.p.A., Milano

Manufactured in the United States and printed on
acid-free paper. The paper used in this publication meets
the minimum requirements of ANSI/NISO Z39.48 1992
(R 1997) (*Permanence of Paper*).

FIRST AMERICAN EDITION

LIBRARY OF CONGRESS CATALOGING-IN-PUBLICATION DATA

Pera, Marcello, 1943-
[Perché dobbiamo dirci cristiani. English]
Why we should call ourselves Christians: the religious roots of
free societies/by Marcello Pera; translated by L.B. Lappin.
p. cm.
Includes bibliographical references (p.) and index.
ISBN-13: 978-1-59403-564-7 (hardcover: alk. paper)
ISBN-10: 1-59403-564-4 (hardcover: alk. paper) 1. Liberalism—
Religious aspects—Catholic Church. 2. Christianity and politics.
3. Liberalism—Europe. 4. Apologetics. I. Title.
BX1396.2.P4713 2011
261.7094—dc23

2011024453

CONTENTS

FOREWORD

Marcello Pera is a senator of the Republic of Italy, who served as president of the Italian Senate during a legislative period. He considers himself a "liberal" (a modern secular thinker) who, however, precisely as such, sees himself within the tradition of Christian thought. His particular area of interest as a philosopher and man of politics is the encounter between the tradition of Christian (Catholic) thought and that of liberal thought. In this book, Pera presents the inner connection between the traditions of Christian and liberal thought, which is critically important for the political and cultural future of Europe. In an impressive way, Pera analyzes the writings of the great liberal thinkers and comes to the surprising conclusion that among the characteristics of liberal thought is its foundation in the Christian image of

God. The emphasis on the idea of man's freedom, characteristic of liberal thought, presupposes the idea of man in the image of God, the consequence of which is precisely the freedom of man. With great scholarly rigor, Pera shows, through an analysis of texts and a presentation of the inner structure of liberalism, that liberalism loses its foundation and thus destroys itself when it abandons this underpinning—the Christian image of God and of man. From here, the title of the book becomes understandable: without its rootedness in the essential elements of the Christian heritage, liberalism loses itself. Liberal democracy in its philosophical foundation presupposes this patrimony and rests upon it.

In this connection, there are also his reflections on the crisis in ethics, in which Pera shows how liberal ethical thought has an inner relationship to the Christian doctrine of the good and how they both can and must be fully linked one to the other on behalf of man.

In light of these essential, fundamental theses of his book, one can understand his analysis of multiculturalism. Pera demonstrates how this concept is in contradiction with itself and how it therefore cannot point the way to the future. Openness to the multifarious cultural patrimony of humanity presupposes one's own cultural identity; only in this way can there be a fruitful encounter among cultures. This is also the case for his analysis of the concepts of interreligious and intercultural dialogue. The reader may be surprised at first that Pera holds that interreligious dialogue, in the strict sense of the word, is not possible, while at the same time he greatly stresses the need for intercultural dialogue. How should we understand this? Pera seeks to argue that, for true believers, the essential faith decisions are not open to discussion. The question, for example, of whether God is or is not triune is not in the final analysis a subject for discussion; on this issue, the yes or no that one gives to the question is a decision taken in faith. Certainly, one can try to explain the inner logic of this apparently contradictory vision and clarify misunderstandings and erroneous interpretations; however, the yes or no as such is not a subject for discussion. But of course one can and must pursue sincere dialogue regarding the ethical and cultural consequences of such fundamental religious decisions in order to attain, in the diversity of these fundamental decisions, the possibility of responsible common action.

With its sober rationality, ample philosophical sophistication, and the force of its argumentation, Pera's book is, in my opinion, of great significance at this moment in the history of Europe and the world. I hope that it will find a broad reception in the United States as well as elsewhere and that it will be helpful in giving the political debate on transitory questions that depth without which we cannot hope to overcome the challenges of our particular historical moment.

Pope Benedict XVI
Castel Gandolfo
September 8, 2009

INTRODUCTION
When Our House Catches Fire

Why should we call ourselves Christians? At first glance, there are myriad reasons for not doing so, because religion today is on trial, accused by many witnesses and condemned by many juries. There are historians who consider it a cultural vestige of a remote epoch; philosophers who relegate it among the primitive forms of knowledge and reflection; scientists who dismiss it as a superseded phase in the evolution of the human species; jurists who oppose it as an obstacle to peaceful social coexistence. As for politicians, they either preach syncretism of all religions ("dialogue" is their word for it) or simply don't believe in anything at all. In every influential arena, today's watchword is "we are all post-religious." Those with religious faith may cultivate it in private if they wish. They can manifest their sentiments and feelings and display their symbols at home, but they are not allowed to speak out at school or in the universities or parliaments, in the streets or in the mass media. Gone are the days of the *agora,* where our Greek forefathers invoked the gods. Today our public spaces must be as aseptic as hospital operating rooms, uncontaminated by the germs of any "conception of the good." States must be independent of religious creeds; politics must take a neutral stance on religious values; societies must hold together without any references to religious or ethical ties.

Of all the religions, Christianity is the one most opposed today, for both general and specific reasons. The general reason is that Christianity was the religious core of the West when it thought of itself as a great vehicle and custodian of civilization. If the West today keeps on beating its breast over its presumed guilt from the past and does not believe itself to be better than other civilizations, then Christianity will also lose its special role. The specific reason is the claim that Christianity and its churches, in particular the Roman Catholic Church, continually impeded scientific, technological, political, and social progress. Does it not still reject the main tenets of modernity and, even more, of postmodernity?

These opinions are so widespread nowadays among the intellectual and political elite of the West that they are taken as the undeniable truth. Luckily, many ordinary people have begun to smell the stink of smoke and to challenge the dominant trend of thought. I am one of those people. My view is that the West today is undergoing a profound moral and spiritual crisis, due to a loss of faith in its own worth, exacerbated by the apostasy of Christianity now rife within Western culture.

I consider myself a liberal, but a word of clarification is in order.

When crossing the Atlantic, one experiences the unsettling phenomenon known to philosophers as "meaning variance": some words do not have the same connotation or denotation on both sides of the ocean. "Liberalism" and "liberal" are words that mean something different, if not completely opposite, between one coast and the other. It's clearly not a question of linguistics, but of history. In Europe, liberals favor the limiting of governmental powers, the autonomy of civil society, and the noninterference of the state in the market. They promote intermediary institutions and prize individual liberty above all. In America, liberals today either oppose all these freedoms or favor restricting and regimenting them for "the common good." In Europe, where the state is *padre padrone* (father and master), liberals see it as an adversary. In America, where the state was traditionally viewed as a necessary evil, liberals now often see it as an ally. Politically speaking, liberals in Europe tend to the right, while in America they tend to the left. The European equivalent for the American term "liberal" is "socialist," while the American equivalent for the European term "liberal" is "conservative."

In the past, Europeans and Americans employed the same expressions without fear of being misunderstood. They began from the same philosophical premise, the doctrine according to which man possesses rights prior to, and independent of, his belonging to a political community, nation, or state. The European philosophers Locke and Kant expressed themselves in exactly the same way as Thomas Jefferson and John Adams: man came into the world "endowed" with unalienable rights.

Endowed by whom? No one had any doubts about this: man had been endowed by God. By what God? No one hesitated here either: by the Christian God, or more precisely, the

Judeo-Christian God, for it was the Judeo-Christian God who created man in his image, and the Christian God who became man and endured suffering in the human condition. This baptismal act is the historical and conceptual foundation of liberalism. Historical, I say, because the intellectual and political battle of liberalism against the old social hierarchies and despotisms—including the alliance of throne and altar—was fought and won by adopting a Christian political theology. Conceptual, I say, because this political theology, explicitly or implicitly, offers the best tools to justify the dignity of man and, as a consequence, the concept of human rights.

This is my philosophical frame of reference. I am interested more in intellectual and cultural questions than in ordinary political issues. When I discuss the latter it is because I believe they can shed light on the former. My overall view, which I will argue here, is that if we remove the Christian underpinnings from human rights, not only will liberal doctrine collapse, but Western civilization will fall along with it. This would be a catastrophic event, but it wouldn't be the first time. Europe has already collapsed in the recent past, when it turned from Christian to pagan or materialist. At the time, great liberal thinkers recognized that Europe's descent into hell had been precipitated or promoted by the rejection of religion and of Christian ethics.

At the outbreak of the Second World War, Karl Popper wrote, "our Western civilization owes its rationalism, its faith in the rational unity of man and in the open society, and especially its scientific outlook, to the ancient Socratic and Christian belief in the brotherhood of all men."[1] Midway through the war, when it seemed that the Nazi hordes were on the verge of overwhelming our Western civilization, the Italian philosopher Benedetto Croce wrote a powerful and influential essay in which he explained "why we cannot help calling ourselves Christians."[2]

When the war was finally won, another great liberal thinker, Friedrich von Hayek, stated that he was "convinced that unless this breach between true liberal and religious convictions can be healed there is no hope for a revival of liberal forces."[3] Note that these thinkers were not Christian believers or men of faith in the strict sense. Also note that they did not say what the illiberal Martin Heidegger would later affirm: "only a god can save us."[4] Rather, they held that Christianity (*our God*) had shaped the West and a return to Christianity could still save it.

Today, politically speaking, liberals have won for the most part. The West has liberal constitutions, liberal institutions, liberal economies, and liberal systems of education. But we are so far from "the end of history" that the same breach between liberalism and Christianity that shook our civilization a few generations ago is now presenting itself in a new form. Not in the violent forms of Nazism or communism, but in the form of liberal secularism. For the destinies of Europe and the West, this ideology is no less dangerous; it is rather more insidious. It does not wear the brutal face of violence, but the alluring smile of culture. With its words, liberal secularism preaches freedom, tolerance, and democracy, but with its deeds it attacks precisely that Christian religion which prevents freedom from deteriorating into license, tolerance into indifference, democracy into anarchy.

This is what is going on especially in Europe. Is America any different? Like all old-school European liberals, I always looked to the American experiment, founded on the myth of a "city on the hill" or a "nation under God," as the best antidote to European philosophical and political infatuations. America was both a goal and a protective shield: Jefferson, Adams, Lincoln, and several other American heroes against Rousseau, Hegel, Marx, and many other European wizards.

Unfortunately, visiting America today I would not be able to draw the same optimistic conclusions that Tocqueville did in writing *Democracy in America.* For example, I am not convinced that this still holds true: "in France [that is, Europe] I had almost always seen the spirit of religion and the spirit of freedom pursuing courses diametrically opposed to each other; but in America I found that they were intimately united, and that they reigned in common over the same country."[5] Surely there are still significant differences between Europe and America, and America is still a pillar of civilization. But I fear the exportation of Europe to America, and I fear that the entire West is in the process of transforming itself into one great secular Europe: still rich and powerful, yet increasingly arid and uninspired by any sense of a moral mission to accomplish.

In addition to being liberal, I also consider myself secular. But here too a clarification is in order, because we are dealing with another major case of meaning variance. Today, "secular" refers to something quite different from its meaning yesterday.

Traditional secularism, like classical liberalism, knew that it owed its origins and foundations to Christian theology because it was Christianity that first invented, long before it practiced, the division between Caesar and God, throne and altar, the City of Man and the City of God. Despite its stern guardianship of the "wall of separation," this secularism did not hesitate to employ the language of Thomas Jefferson: "Can the liberties of a nation be thought secure when we have removed their only firm basis, a conviction in the minds of the people that these liberties are of the gift of God? That they are not to be violated but with his wrath?"[6] Or the language of John Adams: "Religion and virtue are the only foundations, not only of republicanism and of all free government, but of social felicity under all governments and in all combinations of human society."[7] Or the similar language of Locke, Kant, Tocqueville, and many others. This is the secularism of which I approve. It opposes theocracy, the submission of the state to ecclesiastical hierarchies, and the interference of churches with democratic decisions. It does not oppose religion, nor does it take Christianity as a fairy tale for the unintellectual.

Today's secularism is different. It views religion as an obstacle to coexistence, science, technology, progress, and human well-being. As Richard Rorty has put it, "in its ideal form, the culture of liberalism would be one which was enlightened, secular, through and through. It would be one in which no trace of divinity remained."[8] This "ideal" entails serious risks that we have already encountered firsthand, because traditional secularism created an open society (especially in America), whereas today's secularism, in spite of its best intentions, is reducing our states to arenas of religious conflict (especially in Europe). Secularism is not producing more peaceful coexistence in our societies, but the contrary.

Consider how secularism confronts Islamic fundamentalism. If the West has not yet found a solution to this problem, it is because it feels guiltier about the idea of "exporting religion" than about using force. Those who believe they have no special position to defend, but only interests to protect, do not even understand the antisecular motives of the fundamentalists or their distaste for our aversion to religion. Or consider how secular liberals tackle the challenge of integrating Muslim citizens into Western societies. If Europe is far from a solution to this problem as well, that is because it no longer believes in its own basic values and is unwilling to demand fidelity to them. Those who preach the relativity of values have renounced their own identity. The bitter truth is that the West is afraid of Islam because it is afraid of religion, and of its own religion first of all.

The title of this book takes after the title of the essay I have already quoted by Benedetto Croce, "Why We Cannot Help Calling Ourselves Christians." In due course I will explain the philosophical reasons that induced Croce to choose a reductive formula for his title and why I cannot accept them. But there is one point I need to clarify from the very beginning: by "Christian" I mean *"Judeo-Christian."* The core idea is that from the viewpoint of both Judaism and Christianity man is created in God's image and likeness. In my opinion, this is the religious source of the concepts of personhood and human dignity, the foundation of the liberal view that man has primacy over society and the state, and the basis for the doctrine of natural, fundamental, individual rights. It is not by chance that when Nazi Europe turned anti-Christian, it also became anti-Semitic. The fact that Christianity, and Catholicism in particular, turned anti-Semitic many a time over the centuries cannot hide the fact that the two faiths are, or may be considered, twin brothers with respect to the conceptual foundations of liberalism.

Each of the three chapters of this book contains an answer to the problem posed in the title.

In the first chapter I will point out the philosophical, cultural, and political reasons why we should call ourselves Christians. In brief: we should call ourselves Christians if we want to maintain our liberties and preserve our civilization. I will challenge the "secular equation" according to which "liberal" is an equivalent term for "non-Christian," or "anti-Christian." A legacy of the Enlightenment and the French Revolution, this equation still hangs like a millstone around our necks. By referring to the philosophical fathers of liberalism, I will also show the conceptual links and the "family resemblance" between liberalism and Christianity.

In the second chapter I will use Europe as a negative case study. If, as Jefferson claimed, our liberties must have, or must be felt as if they had, a religious foundation in order to bind the nation together, then today's secularized Europe, which rejects that foundation, can never be politically united. Nor are there any efficacious surrogates for a religious or ethical foundation. As I will try to demonstrate, Habermas's "constitutional patriotism" (just like Rawls' "nonmetaphysical" liberalism) can constitute politically unifying and binding elements only after a *pre*-political basis has been established. If such a basis does not exist, or if it is rejected, any effort to build a European nation or a European super-state is doomed to fail. The fact is that, unlike Americans, Europeans cannot adopt a constitution beginning with the words "We the people," because "the people" must exist as a moral and spiritual community *before* such a constitution could be conceived and asked for. But as a spiritual and moral community, "the people" cannot exist unless it first recognizes that the fundamental rights and freedoms knitting it together are not concessions inscribed in a juridical document, but are, to use Jefferson's words again, the gift of God, or the result of our efforts to become worthy of the gift. Such an acknowledgment is precisely what is not happening in Europe.

In the third chapter I will examine the down-sliding of our liberal states. Secularism, scientism, relativism, multiculturalism are bringing about a moral decline. Liberal civilization was born in defense of the negative liberties of man. When the positive liberties of citizen burgeoned forth, everything started changing. The liberal state first became democratic, next paternalistic, and finally entered the totalitarian phase of the dictatorship of the majority and the tyranny of absolute authorities. No aspect of life today, from cradle to grave, has been left untouched by legislation, and most of all by the verdicts of judges or supreme courts, or by the decisions of supranational institutions. The moral sphere—once entrusted to the wisdom of the family, parish, and local community, carefully kept separate from the political sphere—is now subjected to proliferating laws and regulations. The outcome is that ethics has been expropriated by the state, and since there always comes a time when expropriators are themselves expropriated, democratic states are now finding that their decisional authority has been handed over to power and interest groups and to bureaucracies. If ethics is drained of all truth, as secularists and relativists maintain, what is good and what is evil are to be determined by parliamentary vote. Or worse.

This book is one of many to come out of September 11. That day, rather than looking at "them," I found myself concentrating on "us," on our civilization, its foundations, its history, its worth, its wrongs as well, but most of all on the reasons why we should appreciate and defend it. This is why I am indebted to countless individuals whom I do not know personally but whose voices have begun to be heard beyond the cage where the reigning orthodoxy is trying to confine them. I am particularly beholden to Benedict XVI, who is not only a pope of the Catholic Church, but a great theologian and scholar, a man of dialogue, and a mild-mannered though resolute person. Words are powerless to express my personal and intellectual gratitude to him.

Writing this book filled an urgent intellectual need of my own. The answer came partly from my political experience, but it could not have been completed without Benedict XVI's appeal to what he, following Toynbee, called "creative minorities."[9] The exceptional circumstance that the pope wished to read this book while it was still in manuscript form and the even more exceptional circumstance that he has written a preface to it far surpass my stature and the merit of my work. These circumstances signify that there are serious problems regarding the destiny of Christianity and of our civilization—and that *all* of us must take these problems to heart.

Last but not least, a word of warning. This book was written for a wide public that is patient enough to confront difficult and delicate problems, as well as for scholars humble enough to look out the window and not just glance over at the desks of colleagues. I ask my nonspecialist readers to bear with me when I dwell on technical issues, and I apologize to my scholarly colleagues if, in treating some of these issues, I have not always used the sophisticated analytical tools of the philosopher's trade.

I do not ask my readers to take my solutions as the only ones worth considering, but to reflect on the problems that I discuss here. It makes no difference whether we are liberals, believers, Christians, Europeans, Americans. What matters is whether we are willing to address these problems or not. I believe that when our house catches fire, we all ought to pitch in to help extinguish the flames.

* * *

The work for the American version of this book has benefited much from the support of the National Endowment for the Humanities. The generosity of the Hudson Institute in Washington, D.C., enabled me to spend time in an intellectually stimulating atmosphere where I had the good fortune to discuss my ideas with colleagues and scholars. I am grateful to both institutions.

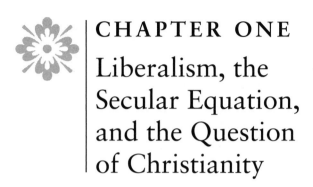

CHAPTER ONE

Liberalism, the Secular Equation, and the Question of Christianity

LIBERALISM AT THE CROSSROADS

The hardest question for liberals to answer nowadays is this: *What is liberalism?*

Whenever a widely accepted doctrine comes up against serious obstacles and must adapt itself to new challenges, the doctrine no longer resembles its original form. It becomes complex and composite, often eclectic. It may have spawned many different versions of itself. But as long as its core is protected, it will continue to be accepted by the competent community. That is the situation of liberalism today.

In terms of political culture, liberals and their kindred have become the governing class of the Western world almost without exception. They have triumphed over absolutism and totalitarianism. They have helped prevent democracy from becoming "the tyranny of the majority," by obliging it to respect certain fundamental human rights and institutions. Liberal regimes are the most advanced in the world, offering greater well-being, opportunity, social mobility, and freedom. Though often beset by economic crises, liberal governments usually manage to overcome them without lowering their citizens' standard of living. They are a beacon for other countries and a goal for refugees and immigrants. Yet this victory of liberal regimes is not in itself "liberal." These regimes today are *hybrids*, especially insofar as liberalism progressively yields to democracy, in which law is produced through majority parliamentary vote concerning even those very rights that liberals regard as fundamental.

Liberal doctrine is also hybrid. There are so many divisions, differences, and fractures within it that we can hardly speak of it as a single doctrine. All its main tenets are subject to controversy. Is liberalism only a political doctrine whose range of action is limited to the organizing of the public sphere, or is it a "comprehensive" doctrine—philosophical, ethical, and metaphysical? When we speak of freedom, the pillar of liberalism, do we mean freedom from coercion, interference, restrictions, etc., or do we mean freedom to lead one's own life in rational and moral autonomy? By "autonomy" do we mean the freedom to make choices according to our own plans, or also the possession of the resources and effective power to do so? Are liberty and private property, or liberty and capitalist economy conceptually related? Are they the same thing? Are they essential to each other, or can they be separated? Are liberty and social justice compatible? How far can a liberal regime tolerate the interference of politics in the state's redistribution of resources? Is liberalism a universal theory, or does it hold good only for certain communities or for ones that have reached a certain stage of human development? Is liberalism blind to all differences among individuals and communities, or is it pluralistic, allowing for ethnic and group rights?

There are no clear-cut answers to any of these questions today, for there are different ways of being "liberal." The upshot is that all current versions of liberalism include various concepts—such as tradition, nation, social justice, redistribution, public intervention—that originated with one or the other of two political families in perpetual competition with each other: conservatism and socialism. Because the elements of liberalism have sprung predominantly from the latter, however, the word "liberal" in American political language has become synonymous with the word "social-democratic" in European political language. Whenever we must add an adjective to the name of a doctrine in order to define it—such as "social" liberalism, "democratic" liberalism, "conservative" liberalism, "libertarian" liberalism, "national" liberalism, "multicultural" liberalism, or, vice versa, "liberal" socialism, "liberal" democracy, and the like—we know that the doctrine itself is imperiled. In the end, it must be reborn in a new guise, or else become obsolete.

Hybrid regimes built on irreconcilable political concepts and a hybrid doctrine composed of incompatible notions both signify the current *crisis of liberalism*. No one denies that this crisis exists, and the very proliferation of schools of thought, variants of doctrine, and research programs are enough to bring even the most obstinate liberal back to reality. But "crisis" does not mean "end" or "demise." The vital core of liberalism remains powerfully resilient and attractive. This core is the idea of natural rights (also known as "human," "fundamental," "essential," or "basic" rights): all human beings are free and equal by nature; their basic liberties exist *prior to* and *independent of* the state, and are *noncoercible by* the state.[1] This idea has various corollaries. One is that every individual is free to pursue his own conception of the good. Another is that everyone enjoys freedom of conscience and religion.

The optimism for which liberals are renowned shines forth in these corollaries. How is it possible for free and equal persons to live together, faithful and loyal to the state, if everyone is authorized to live as he pleases, and is thus potentially in conflict with everyone else? We must presuppose that in order to guarantee social coexistence, liberal societies must be able to harmonize all their conceptions of the good (or maintain a minimum distance among them all) and to ensure maximum compatibility among religious faiths (or maintain a minimum of friction among them). Otherwise, the war of all against all would ensue—precisely that wild state of nature that liberals aspire to supersede—with lethal outcome for the whole of society.[2]

The great fathers of liberalism were well aware of this problem and were confident it could be solved. To this end, they invented "cosmopolitan law," "federation of states," and "perpetual peace," just as their descendants have invented the United Nations, the International Court of Justice, and the Universal Declaration of Human Rights. But history has shaken even the most deep-seated convictions. In terms of doctrine, liberal presuppositions have been shaken by the discovery of the plurality of values, and even more so by the idea of the incommensurability of values, i.e. that there is no common measure with which all the forms of culture and civilization may be evaluated. In terms of policies, liberal regimes are endangered in modern societies, beleaguered by the re-emergence of strong nationalistic sentiments, by increased friction among various conceptions of the good, and by the spreading of multiculturalism, the idea that groups, classes, or categories may have special rights distinct from those of the majority or from those of humanity as a whole. It is no wonder that the old liberal belief in the moral and rational unity of mankind—the brotherhood of man—has fragmented to such an extent today that it has become a paradox, as expressed in the motto of the European Union, "Unity in Diversity."

Religion, in particular, resists liberal optimism. Bouncing boldly back into the limelight, it poses questions of identity and belonging, and is at once the obstacle to the integration and coexistence of millions of immigrants, and the stimulus for the forming of new states. It has limited or bogged down legislation in the field of ethics, generated fundamentalism and created friction, violence, even terrorism. As a result, in the liberal West, the terms of the question have changed. Regarding the exercise and justification of liberal rights, our society has been transformed from a homogeneous one shaped by Christian values (as it was for centuries) into one marked by intense religious conflict.

To avoid or minimize this conflict, liberals have offered two remedies: to oppose religion outright, or to separate it from public life. These two very different solutions converge in the equation "liberal = secular." In this view, secularity is viewed as a shield protecting the core of the liberal doctrine. If society is secular and the state is also secular, then, to cite an example of liberal optimism, religion cannot penetrate it, and thus religion poses no threat to social stability.

Although this idea is so widely held that it is treated as a sort of dogma, it has not yielded satisfactory results, especially in Europe. On the contrary, it has worsened the moral or ethical-civil crisis that Europe is now undergoing, just at the time when "giving Europe a soul" has become politically imperative in order to safeguard the great plan of a United Europe. Thus the second hardest question for liberals to answer nowadays is this: *What is the relationship between liberalism and religion?*— if indeed there is one—and more specifically, *between liberalism and Christianity,* which is the religious tradition of the founding fathers of liberalism and of the liberal Western countries? This is the crossroads where liberal doctrine stands today, and where its destiny will be played out. The answer to this question is vital. If there is indeed a non-extrinsic link between liberalism and Christianity, then liberalism may rely on a solid heritage of ethical and religious values as an anchor for the basic concepts of its own doctrine. If no such link exists, then liberalism is doomed to become the propagator of its own crisis.[3]

Standing at this crossroads, I take the first road. I reject the illiberal positions that have been the disastrous intellectual and political exercise of so many fascists, Nazis, and communists.[4] I also reject the antiliberal positions held by many conservatives, even though I do believe that conservatism is right on one point often neglected by liberalism today: the need to defend the founding principles of our own tradition. Most specifically, I do not share the objection that the doctrine of liberalism is based on individualism, egoism, hedonism, or that it is unconcerned with virtue and the common good.[5] I also reject that philosophy of history, deriving from Hegel and Heidegger, according to which modernity begins with the birth of individualism in the sixteenth century; proceeds through the scientific revolution in the seventeenth, the Enlightenment in the eighteenth, the birth of nationalism in the nineteenth; and ends in the twentieth with Auschwitz and the gulag, after which "only a god can save us." Such an account of history has been put forward precisely by those antiliberals and anti-Christians who, after the tragedy to which they themselves lent a hand, now beat their breasts and continue to pray to the wrong divinity ("*a* god," but never *our* God), or believe that to stop praying and to deprive religion of any meaning and value is the best remedy for our moral disease.

There are many objections to liberalism, and some of them are reasonable and well founded.[6] My complaint is that liberalism has lost faith in its own founding principles and has severed the historical and conceptual ties that once linked it to Christianity. I am convinced that some ideas prevalent among liberals today—for example, that religion should not voice opinions, that it is irrelevant to public life, that it is an obstacle, or that it has become outmoded in the modern or postmodern world— are indefensible in theory and disastrous in practice, especially in Europe, where the crisis of liberalism is most keenly felt.[7] This is the thesis I will be defending.

Before I proceed, I would like to make it clear that, given the theoretically and politically hybrid nature of my subject, I will be discussing liberalism, liberals, and liberal regimes from a philosophical and cultural rather than a strictly political point of view.[8] In order to avoid interfering in tormented family quarrels, and to push aside the unsolvable purist controversies ("Who is an *authentic* liberal?" "What is *real* liberalism?"), whenever I must resort to other authors I will refer to those who have defined themselves as liberals or to those in whom the core of the liberal doctrine is visibly at work. The problem we are dealing with here, the relationship between liberalism and religion, will assist us, because it is on this ground that the similarities are most starkly drawn. For example, despite the differences for which liberal Americans are considered "left-wing" and liberal Europeans "right-wing," the critical and negative perspective on religion they share places both on the same side, holding similar theoretical views on the issue and tending to favor similar political measures.

The main theater of my inquiry in this chapter stretches from Europe out to the entire West. To set the stage, I will begin with the apostasy of Christianity that is widespread on the Old Continent and that is being cultivated today by liberal and secular culture. I will then address four points. First, I will present and argue against the equation "liberal = secular" as it is currently maintained by liberals. Second, I will survey the history of anticlericalism, of which this equation is a vestige. Third, I will turn to the fathers of liberalism to understand how they treated the problem and to seek inspiration from them. Fourth, I will address the main point: why liberals *should* call themselves Christians. *Should* call themselves, I say, not "can" or "can't help but" call themselves.

THE APOSTASY OF CHRISTIANITY

To manage the tempestuous relations between ethnic groups, cultures, and religions within their societies, European governments have adopted typically liberal policies such as: generous legislation concerning immigration; facilitation in obtaining citizenship; the acceptance of foreign customs that are incompatible with our own; the censoring of the symbols of our own history; the refusal to see religion as a decisive factor in public life or even as an influence on social behavior and custom. In the area of ethics, commonly adopted liberal measures have included the proliferation of so-called "new rights," the recognition of the most diverse and sometimes (at least with respect to our own tradition) perverse demands, and the permissive authorizing of medical research and therapeutic practices that touch the core of basic Christian values.

In implementing these measures, liberal governments and political forces use what seem to be the noblest and most generous words in the political vocabulary: "inclusion," "recognition," "welcoming," "acceptance of minorities," "dialogue," "tolerance," and "respect," as well as "post-national constellation" and "postmodern society," all referring to an ideal type of community without borders: one that is pluralistic and open, indulgent and permissive, bound together by "constitutional patriotism," another expression dear to modern liberals.

The consequences of this mixture of humanitarianism, utilitarianism, subjectivism, and permissiveness have fallen short of expectations. Open-border policies have provoked social friction in some great European cities (including the suburbs of Paris). The welcoming of immigrants has produced no-man's-lands under special jurisdiction that is incompatible with national jurisdiction (in England) and episodes of ethnic and religious violence (in the Netherlands). Multiculturalism and assimilation, the European recipes for integration, have not put an end to incidents of religious conflict but only disguised them. In France, for example, an outcry over the hijab, the veil or headscarf worn by Muslim women, was treated as a debate concerning appropriate dress in public. In Italy, a recent controversy over the removal of crucifixes from schools and other public areas was resolved through recourse to legal technicalities: the supreme court refused to rule on the question when protests arose, claiming it was a matter for local administrations to decide. The idea of the post-national constellation bound together by constitutional patriotism has not stamped out the fires in the hotbeds of the new ethnic nationalisms (in Belgium as in the Balkans). It has failed to protect Europe from Islamic terrorism (in Madrid or London), or to prevent the European Constitution, for which it was elaborated, from running aground (as demonstrated by the negative outcomes of the referendums in France and the Netherlands and more recently in Ireland). The new laws touted as "civil rights victories" have raised serious controversies concerning all major ethical issues.

A boomerang effect has been created in Europe. The more that political leaders proceed on the basis that "we are liberal because we are open, tolerant, permissive, respectful of everyone, and masters of ourselves," the more confused, uncertain, and uneasy citizens feel, and the greater their need for moral and spiritual points of reference, for touchstones of identity. Those needs make the issue of religion all the more pertinent today.

The tradeoff between enjoying the maximum freedom to do as we please and the spiritual letdown that follows, between the championing of freedom at all costs and the paltry results obtained, between the elation of being master of oneself and the sense of insecurity felt by all has deepened Europe's current moral or ethical crisis. The old questions Kant asked himself, "What should I do? What can I hope for?" are being heard today in varying forms on the lips of many, and the vague answers received have provoked despondency, frustration, and loss of confidence—not only on the moral plane, but also at the political, social, and even demographic levels. What is Europe? What is the West? What do they believe in? What ideas and values do they stand for? What lifestyles do they pursue?

Religion is the main cause of this disheartenment. Rather than being neglected, it is openly opposed. What is happening today among the intellectual elite of Western countries, including the United States, is an *apostasy of Christianity.*[9] It is a battle on all fronts, from politics to science, from law to custom, in which the religious tradition that baptized Europe and fostered it for centuries is now accused of threatening the secular state, obstructing social coexistence, and hindering scientific research.

The result is that in a Europe without God, Europeans must coexist without an identity.[10] I will return to this idea, but first I will list the most obvious and telling signs of this apostasy:

Europe has avoided mentioning its Judeo-Christian roots in the European Constitution (dead and buried, briefly resurrected in a new guise, then dead once again).

Europe has excluded a politician from the European Commission because in private life he stated that homosexual marriage goes against his Christian faith.

Europe has promoted legislation that violates Christian principles on major ethical issues. It defends abortion, eugenics, euthanasia, embryonic manipulation. It tolerates polygamy and has lowered legislative defenses against pedophilia.

Europe did not defend a pope, Benedict XVI, from attack after one of his lectures, in which he stated that Christianity is the religion of the *logos* and not of the sword, and asked Islamic leaders to make a similar statement.

Europe barred this same pope from speaking at one of its major universities because it was a public and secular institution.

Europe hides its Christian symbols and discourages the use of religious greetings such as "Merry Christmas" or "Happy Easter," because it does not wish to offend nonbelievers or members of other religions.

In its various states, Europe grants maximum religious liberty and freedom of worship to Muslims but allows this same liberty to be repressed to the point of martyrdom among Christians in Africa, China, Turkey, and India.

Europe invokes freedom of expression to protect artworks that are blasphemous from the Christian point of view, yet suspends this same freedom when dealing with irreverent satire against Islam.

Europe reacts feebly against fundamentalism and Islamic terrorism because it feels guilty about exporting Christian civilization.

And thus, step by step, Europe is surrendering. It is no surprise that scholars now speak of a "Godless Europe,"[11] and that statistics show Europe, the old "Christian continent," to be one of the more secularized areas of the West.[12]

Plato certainly wasn't thinking of Europe in the twenty-first century when he wrote the *Republic,* but the state in which he lived was experiencing a crisis similar to our own, a crisis of which he left a record for posterity. He understood very well what happens when liberty becomes license and democracy disintegrates into anarchy.

In the democratic state, Plato writes, "are they not free? And is not the city chock-full of liberty and freedom of speech? And has not every man license to do as he likes? . . . And where there is such license, it is obvious that everyone would arrange a plan for leading his own life in the way that pleases him. . . . [T]his is the most beautiful of polities; as a garment of many colors, embroidered with all kinds of hues, so this, decked and diversified with every type of character, would appear the most beautiful." (*Republic*, VIII, xi, 557b–c)

This is a perfect portrait of Europe today: alluring ("the most beautiful"), multicultural ("a garment of many colors" that is "decked and diversified with every type of character"), and free ("everyone would arrange a plan for leading his own life"). It is also egalitarian ("assigning a kind of equality indiscriminately to equals and unequals alike," 558c), relativist ("are all alike and to be equally esteemed," 561c), forgiving and mild in the meting out of punishment ("is not the placability of some convicted criminals exquisite?" 558a). It is a place where education is permissive ("the teacher fears and fawns upon the pupils and the pupils pay no heed to the teacher," 563a) and where politically correct language that twists the meaning of ancient words has become the norm ("they euphemistically denominate insolence 'good breeding,' license 'liberty,' prodigality 'magnificence' and shamelessness 'manly spirit,'" 560e–561a).

Yet the society depicted by Plato and our own society are deteriorating. "Is not the avidity of democracy for that which is its definition and criterion of good [that is, liberty] the thing which dissolves it too?" (562b).

The moral crisis of Europe consists in this deterioration: in our politics, no longer believed to be the responsibility of all; in our lifestyle, increasingly tolerant of aberrant behavior and averse to moral restrictions; in our social life, often tainted by self-interest and reduced to the sphere of monads. Liberals are called upon to elaborate a sound, theoretical response to this deterioration, not an eclectic or occasional one. For this they need to agree on a single, consistent position that is politically attractive and morally empowered. Otherwise, liberals may feel proud to have produced the "free society," the "open society," or the "post-traditional society" along with the "consumer society"; they may congratulate themselves on working to bring about "perpetual peace" and a "cosmopolitan society"; but they will not be able to boast that they have built a good, just, or virtuous society. On the contrary, they will have to bear the responsibility of achieving the exact opposite.

THE SECULAR EQUATION

Let's examine the link between liberalism and religion from a doctrinal point of view, calling upon a few representative, influential thinkers. They tend to deny that such a link exists, or to insist that it be severed if it does.

According to John Rawls, the most authoritative liberal voice today, liberalism is "a freestanding political conception,"[13] one that is "not metaphysical" and is "independent of controversial philosophical and religious doctrines,"[14] needing no outside foundation, in particular no comprehensive doctrine of the good, such as religious faith, and accepting no values other than its own political values. Similarly, according to Jürgen Habermas (to name another scholar who, though not exactly liberal, seems to be heading in that direction), liberalism "understands itself as a nonreligious and post-metaphysical justification of the normative bases of the democratic constitutional state," because "the constitution of the liberal state can satisfy its own need for legitimacy in a self-sufficient manner."[15] Richard Rorty writes that the ideal liberal culture "would be one in which no trace of divinity remained."[16] For Bruce Ackerman, the liberal state is "deprived of divine revelation."[17] Many other liberals think that the main tenet of liberalism consists in the rejection of religion, or in the idea that it is irrelevant or useless.[18]

Why do they say this?

The reason is a single idea that has put down roots and grown to be dominant among liberals. Politicians, intellectuals, historians, philosophers, writers, journalists, analysts—the cultural mainstream responsible for shaping public opinion—agree that liberalism implies or equals secularism. "Liberal = secular" is the prevalent dogma wherever power is exercised: schools, universities, parliaments, the media. I call this formula "the secular equation," and those formulas deriving from it or connected to it are "secular equations." Translated into political terms and applied to the state, this means:

1) The liberal state is secular.

Although this equation is so commonly held as to be almost undisputed, perhaps for this very reason its meaning is not immediately clear. "Secular" is an ambiguous term. It can be construed in the sense of "that which is not justified or argued in terms of religious belief," or "that which is justified in terms differing from or opposed to those of religious belief." In the former connotation, "secular" refers to persons or entities that stand apart from religion. In the latter, it refers to persons or entities that deny or oppose religion. Taken in the former meaning, the secular equation becomes:

2) The liberal state is nonreligious.

Understood correctly, in the strictest sense, this formula is true, and more precisely it has become true for us today. After the end of absolutism and the separation of throne from altar, we all consider it a great political victory that the institutions of the state are an open house where everyone can coexist with everyone else and no one feels discriminated against or excluded because of his religious faith. In our post-Westphalian epoch, the principle of *cuius regio eius religio* (same state, same religion) would be inconceivable. By its very nature, the liberal state does not interfere with the free choices of its citizens. It imposes no religious creed and submits to no ecclesiastical authority ("free church in a free state"). Even where state churches exist or where a certain faith is affirmed to be the religion of the majority of the population, that dictate of law is an inert historical vestige imposing no special religious obligations.

The second equation has a marked characteristic: it is negative. We can see why this is a defect if we ponder particular circumstances that often arise in our pluralistic regimes. What is to be done when citizens divide themselves into competing religious groups over certain public issues, and then turn to the state to settle their differences? In order to obtain an answer, we need to transform the negative formula into a positive one and determine *how* the state must behave. But before that, we need to determine *if* the state must assume a certain position or even make a decision at all. Liberals have been inspired by the principle that the state must be *independent* from and *neutral* toward religious beliefs. However, since this principle is negative and doesn't say if the state should act in particular circumstances or what it should do, liberal thinkers have offered further explanation:

If the principle of neutrality obliges the state to refrain from intervening in religious matters, and citizens nevertheless ask the state to take a position that may have religious repercussions, then the state, in order to safeguard its neutrality and at the same time satisfy its citizens' requests, may be required to dictate certain *public political norms* of a secular, national, or otherwise nonreligious kind that meet with maximum consensus or minimum dissent. For the rest, it will allow its citizens complete freedom of religious faith *in private*. Thus, the state will not have to decide which religious creed should prevail over another, but rather what demands from religious groups are compatible with its public political norms. The state remains neutral from a religious point of view, but not passive when called upon to make political decisions. This is Rawls' main principle of *political* liberalism.[19] Seen in this positive light, the equation becomes:

3) The liberal state transfers religion to the private sphere, or the liberal state excludes religion from the public sphere.

This is the formula of contemporary political liberalism, whose substance consists in distinguishing and separating (public) "political conceptions" from (private) "comprehensive doctrines of the good." When Rawls and Habermas say that liberalism is "self-sufficient," they mean that it is neither based on, nor requires justification from, any other pre-political doctrine, whether ethical, philosophical, metaphysical, or religious. Furthermore, they mean that liberalism distinguishes and separates the public sphere (nonreligious) from the private spheres (religious or other).[20] Naturally, to the citizen who finds his faith marginalized or shoved into a ghetto, this might seem like a sacrifice, a renunciation, or even a form of violence, but he is told that it is actually a great advantage because it prevents or reduces conflicts that might occur in conditions of pluralism, and thus averts even worse episodes of violence.

So that's fine, right? No. Despite its excellent intentions, this view, in its crudely literal form, has serious flaws. First, since there is no external authority to draw the line between public and private, whoever does draw that line must do so from *within* his own culture, where it is impossible to eliminate every religious creed or comprehensive doctrine. Furthermore, religious beliefs by their very nature have a public dimension and are intended to guide public decisions. Professing a faith is not like wearing a certain set of pajamas to bed or a special tie at a reception, where tastes and fashions are inconsequential. Those who follow a faith draw life teachings and guidance from that faith, not only for their own lives but also for those of others; thus it is impossible to ask them to confine their faith to the private sphere unless they are coerced to do so. Finally, history has shown that very often the conventional wisdom of one era was the comprehensive doctrine of the preceding age. Consider the major liberal political victories. For example, a constitution that declares equal dignity and guarantees equal rights to men and women affirms a political standpoint held by everyone nowadays, but it also contains elements of a comprehensive ethical doctrine that in the past was endorsed by only a few groups (who fought against discrimination). Naturally, there is reason to believe that political liberalism cannot be confined within the limits of a neutral or procedural conception, but is itself a comprehensive doctrine or part of one.[21]

I will return to this point later. Here I would like to stress that the very same liberals who introduced the third formula understood how crude it was and tried to correct it. Rawls, for one, watered it down with a "proviso": comprehensive doctrines can be introduced into the public sphere *provided that* public reasons are given for them over the course of time.[22] Habermas diluted it further with an "institutional translation proviso": religious doctrines can be introduced into public discussion *provided that* they are argued in rational terms.[23]

These and other similarly weakened versions of the third formula[24] make absolutely good sense. Both exclude dogmatic arguments from the public sphere, such as: "That's how it has to be because my God wants it that way," or "That's how it has to be because that's what the scripture of my religion says."[25] But even though good sense may be a major pragmatic ingredient of every act of the state upon which the peaceful coexistence of our societies largely depends, it still leaves a few very delicate problems unsolved.

Consider the case of bioethical controversies, such as when someone says, "I am against abortion because according to my religion it violates the sacred principle of life," or, "I am against euthanasia because according to my faith it injures the dignity of the human person." Since it would be illiberal to prevent anyone from expressing such opinions in the public sphere, a reply must be given. But what reply? Here the liberal state finds itself in an awkward dilemma. If it makes a decision, either affirmative or negative, it settles a controversy but also endorses or rejects a particular religious doctrine (the doctrine professing the inviolability of life and of the human person). In that case, however, it is no longer a secular state because it has not upheld the secular equation. If it refrains from making a decision and allows its citizens the freedom to be guided by their own conscience, then the state cannot be said to have endorsed any particular religious doctrine, but the controversy remains unsettled. In that case, it is no longer a liberal state willing to answer its citizens' demands for justice. It has upheld the liberal equation, but it has done so to the detriment of its own authority and of the coexistence between groups in conflict.

Is there a way out of this dilemma? One of many solutions proposed is this: the liberal state is, indeed, neutral and independent as to religious beliefs, but this neutrality is based on clearly understood and shared values; that is, "the secular state is not empty."[26] Here we find the second meaning of the term "secular" previously mentioned: that which is justified in terms different from or opposed to religious terms. This means that the liberal state does not endorse any particular religious or comprehensive doctrine (otherwise it would no longer be secular); rather, it endorses its *own* religious or comprehensive doctrine. In this case, the secular equation becomes:

4) The liberal state professes a secular religion.

Here, "secular" is to be understood not only negatively, as that which "consists of freeing the public sphere from any influence exercised in the name of a particular religion or ideology," but also positively, as that which "embodies the simultaneous choice of freedom of conscience and equality."[27] That we are dealing here with a religion is proved by the fact that the state expresses this "choice" only in a pre-political sphere, as a baptismal act of its being a liberal state. In other words, the "choice of freedom of conscience and equality" must be upheld by a *faith* that people must *believe in* as a preliminary presupposition and necessary condition of their citizenship.

Typically, although not exclusively, this is the French for-mula, which in politics defends French assimilationism, and in doctrine belongs to the secularism enshrined in the modern his-tory of France and in its constitution. Yet the fourth equation is no better than the previous ones. If anything, it is worse.

In France, problems arose during the much-publicized con-troversy over the hijab, the veil or headscarf worn by Muslim women (an issue felt even more keenly in Turkey). The question was: should Muslim girls be allowed to wear the hijab—or more generally, should religious symbols be displayed—in schools and other public places? The Stasi Commission appointed by the French government to issue a report on the subject in 2003 said no, because "spiritual and religious petitions cannot bear any influence on the state and must renounce the political dimension. Secularism is not compatible with any conception of religion that claims to regulate, in the name of the principles of the religion itself, the social system or political order." Moreover, "secularism makes a distinction between free spiritual and religious expres-sion in the public sphere, which is legitimate and essential for democratic debate, and influence over it, which is illegitimate."[28]

It may be that in politics this thesis offers a useful compro-mise, a lesser evil in order to avoid a harsher conflict. But in doctrine it contains an obvious contradiction. How is it pos-sible to regard "free expression" of religious beliefs as legiti-mate, but their "influence" as illegitimate? Is it not precisely the goal of free expression to influence public debate and political decisions? By what (secular) miracle is it possible for religious expression to be free yet have no influence? Only one, the mir-acle by which secularism has been transmuted into a religion.

Urging the National Assembly to ban the wearing of Islamic headscarves in public places, on February 3, 2004, the French prime minister, Jean-Pierre Raffarin, stated very clearly, "Today all the great religions in France's history have adapted to this principle [of secularism]. For the most recent arrival, I mean Islam, secularity is an opportunity: the opportunity to be a French religion." Or as many liberals say, "a secular religion."[29]

This oxymoron has created an enormous political mess and can be accepted only if imposed by law. If such an imposition does not make heads roll today as it did in the times when the Goddess Reason was worshipped, it is indeed because good sense is an ingredient in the politics of states, including France, or because, as in this particular case, the French state does not believe in what the French law says, or because it is changing its policies.[30]

To conclude: when we attempt to explain the secular equation, it becomes untenable. In its second and third formulas, it is untenable because it just can't manage to confine religion to the private sphere except through coercion. In its fourth formula, it is untenable either because it contains a contradiction in terms or because it leads to a form of Jacobinism.

Then why do so many people believe in the secular equation?

LIBERALISM AND ANTICLERICALISM

First we must see the secular equation for what it is. Since Christianity is the religion proper to Europe and the West, it is Christianity that liberalism wishes to banish to the private sphere or to oppose as an important religion and public point of reference. The secular equation is intended to be, and indeed is, anti-Christian; more specifically, it is anti-Catholic. It is the learned, polite, attractive, theoretical formulation of the apostasy of Christianity.

We will understand why this is so, and why the secular equation is so widely accepted, if we peek behind it. Behind the equation liberal = secular, we find the tainted vestige of another equation in European culture: liberal = anticlerical. It is the church, and more precisely the temporal role of the church in Europe, that has made a difference, and it is especially the attitudes of and toward the church that have engendered the antagonism between liberalism and Christianity. History tells us so.

Liberalism is a bourgeois movement, and thus a modern one. Its doctrine originated with the demands made by individuals for autonomy and for emancipation from social hierarchies imposed by aristocracies, theocracies, despotism, and absolutism. The development of liberalism has run parallel to capitalism and modern science, and it has produced similar effects. By locating the autonomy of the individual at the center of the social world, liberalism severed the ties of the old alliance between politics and religion. Similarly, by placing the free reason of the individual at the center of scientific research, modern science severed the bonds of the other old alliance: between scientific and religious knowledge.

Both sides challenged the authority of the church, which for centuries had interpreted and watched over those alliances. In the intellectual realm, this authority has been substituted by that of the single individual with his freedom (humanism), of the *ego cogitans* with its ideas (Descartes), of the empirical self with its sensations and passions (Hume), of the transcendental self with its categories (Kant), until it has at last fragmented into phantasmagoria (Nietzsche). In the social realm, the substituting of the church's authority has worked in favor of the new leaders of bourgeois society—the merchant, the craftsman, the banker, the worker, the artist, the intellectual, the technician—until it has become lost in the most extreme anonymity. In order to be free, each person must be personally responsible for his own actions. Locke, writing at the time when liberalism was developing its first great doctrinal formulation, said that men must dispose of themselves "*without* subordination or subjection" to another.[31] Kant, writing a century later when liberalism was challenging absolutism in his country, said that each person "must use one's own understanding *without* the guidance of another."[32] In 1792, Humboldt synthesized the liberal theses of his time (and the secular ones of our time) when he wrote that "the state *has no right* to interfere with the private matters of its citizens as long as the rights of others are not harmed."[33] The motto of the Enlightenment, *dare to know,* elevated the individual from the theoretical point of view. From the practical point of view, it was an invitation to fight for freedom.

The battle of liberalism against the old alliances and against the church as it struggled to preserve them was ruthless and bloody. Since it is well known, or may be regarded as such, I will not elaborate on it here. I wish instead to discuss the attempts made at reconciliation. One of these attempts seems particularly promising today because it entails claiming that the two adversaries are both right. This is the core of the theory concerning the separation of the "religious sphere" from the "political sphere"; of the "realm of faith" from the "realm of science." This theory holds that if the politician keeps to the practical guidance of his state and does not concern himself with the souls of its citizens, and if the scientist respects the rules of his method and does not touch dogmas of faith, there can be no interference. Thus the old classical and medieval alliances were irrevocably broken and the oneness of the ancient cosmos split in two. Subject no longer concurred with object; nor was it only a mirror. The "book of nature" had been unfettered from the "book of scripture." From the evil of this rupture, however, the good of a new victory was born: a great instauration, to use Bacon's term, a door always open so that all those who continually cross its threshold may freely contribute to the advancement of knowledge. *Multi pertransibunt et augebitur scientia.* ("Many shall go to and fro, and knowledge shall be increased.")

Yet again, such optimism is not completely justified. For one of those spheres, the other remains a boundary that cannot be crossed. Bacon set three limitations for science: "the first, that we do not so place our felicity in knowledge as we forget our mortality, the second, that we make application of our knowledge, to give ourselves repose and contentment and not distaste or repining, the third, that we do not presume by the contemplation of nature to attain to the mysteries of God."[34] Or, as we might put it today, we cannot employ scientific knowledge to erode the truth of faith. With respect to politics, Locke, though he acknowledged liberty as a fundamental right, asserted that it had to be exercised *"within* the bounds of the law of nature,"[35] or as we might say, with full respect for ethics or religion.

This means that interference is always possible because the two spheres or orders touch each other and even intersect at certain points. When that happens, both claim to have the right to decide. Thus for the church, as for any Christian believer, the free state can never be so free that it may become the source of all rights and liberties. Free science can never be so free that it may call basic religious values into question.[36] On the other hand, it is hard for the free state to tolerate external limits to its authority, and for free science to recognize any criteria for truth other than its own.

Let us examine a case from the arena of politics and one from that of science. Locke held that "the care of the salvation of men's souls cannot belong to the magistrate,"[37] but did not hesitate to invoke the rigor of the state, in particular against papists and atheists, who "are not at all to be tolerated."[38] Galileo paid homage to the separation of the two spheres, but upon finding himself in their incandescent junction, also claimed that if a result has been rigorously obtained through "sensible experiences and necessary demonstrations," it "*should not in any way* be called into question on account of scriptural passages whose words appear to have a different meaning."[39]

The theory of a free church in a free state and that of a free science alongside a free faith offer a useful compromise, but they are not enough to eliminate conflicts of principle. Indeed, relations grew difficult in principle, even for the best minds. (Think of the relations between Cavour and Pius IX, similar to those between Galileo and Urban VIII.) To the claims made by the church in the name of faith, liberals responded with *anticlericalism.*[40] To the claims made by liberals in the name of freedom, the church responded by raising the flag of *temporalism.* Thus through action and reaction, a dramatic chapter of history unfolded, and today, as a result, liberals and Christians find themselves preassigned to antagonistic roles that they have imbibed with their mothers' milk.

We will limit ourselves here to recalling a few major events in that chapter of history, in accusation and in defense of the church.

The accusations: The church allied itself with absolutism. It defended temporal power. It carried on intestine religious wars. It sided against the birth of some nation-states (France and Italy). It was hostile to Erasmus; an adversary of Galileo; contrary to Beccaria. It opposed freedom of conscience and research (through the institutions of the Inquisition and the Index). It was slow coming to terms with liberal thought, democracy, and capitalism. It was an adversary and persecutor of the Jews. It blessed fascism; did not take a clear and strong stand against Nazism; and now is in danger of failing to understand the risks of Islamism.

The defense: The church supported Europe against those who threatened its identity (Islam). It has been subjected to persecution, expropriation, and violence perpetrated by illuminists and liberals of every kind, by freemasons of every rite and lodge, anticlericals of all varieties, neopagans of every ilk. It has united multitudes of human beings—of different languages, dialects, customs, traditions, and political regimes—within nations and states. It laid the foundation for and gives its support to the culture of the basic rights of man. It has nurtured the birth of popular political parties that have led huge masses of people to "Christian democracy." It has advanced ethical mores, defended the family, fostered education, and aided the poor. It opposed materialism, scientism, and in general that "atheist humanism"[41] which, to cite a few celebrated obituaries, viewed religion as "the opium of the people" (Marx), or dismissed it as "a narcotic with which men control their anguish, but which blunts their minds" (Freud), or regarded the Christian religion in particular as a "slave morality" (Nietzsche), or wished "to send God and the scoundrel philosophers who defend him to the dump heap" (Lenin). And as for hostility toward modernity or slowness in coming to terms with it, the church acted in such a manner in order to protect religion, not to impede "progress."

Does the good outweigh the evil here, or vice versa? Let those endowed with calm judgment draw their conclusions.[42] Let those who find things to criticize go on criticizing as they see fit. But in the end, how can we fail to see that without the Catholic Church, Europe would have disappeared not once but countless times, and that the West would have lost its civilization? How can we fail to realize that Christianity would have been wiped out, and along with it the ethic of love, brotherhood, piety, and charity? How can we fail to understand that the church is also a profane institution, with the virtues and shortcomings of all institutions, but not *solely* an institution? How can we fail to realize that when other institutions, parties, movements, or systems—political, philosophical, juridical, economic—are in error, they simply cease to attract adherents or they disappear, but when the church errs, its very errors exalt the grandeur of its message, the noncontingent value of its words, and the spiritual reality to which it bears witness?

I repeat, everyone is free to draw his own conclusions. But there is one point on which we all ought to agree: the collision between Christianity and liberalism, between the church and modernity produced a fertile outcome for both sides.

In the *Syllabus of Errors,* the annex to the papal encyclical *Quanta Cura,* Pius IX condemned the idea that "the Roman Pontiff can, and ought to, reconcile himself, and come to terms with progress, liberalism and modern civilization." Because of that condemnation, he is still considered the archenemy of liberals. Yet no genuine liberal or scientist today could accept many of the theses he condemned in the *Syllabus of Errors.* Take this statement on positivism: "The State, as being the origin and source of all rights, is endowed with a certain right not circumscribed by any limits." Or take this one regarding scientism: "All the dogmas of the Christian religion are indiscriminately the object of natural science or philosophy, and human reason, enlightened solely in an historical way, is able, by its own natural strength and principles, to attain to the true science of even the most abstruse dogmas; provided only that such dogmas be proposed to reason itself as its object."[43]

Yet a collision did occur, and we are the heirs of its outcome. The dispute between the church and modernity left a spectacle impressed upon our eyes that can best be described by the words of Tocqueville: "the religionists are the enemies of liberty and the friends of liberty attack religion."[44] It has left us with a mannered anticlericalism—instinctive, automatic, dogmatic, like all convictions passed down and accepted without the benefit of critical examination.

We cannot change the facts of history. However, we can discuss, study, and evaluate them, and we can correct the force of intellectual inertia created by those facts. Today with respect to religion, it is necessary that we do so. We can be anticlerical (and we should be if clerical temporalism were to rear its head). We can be secular (and we should be if the separation of church and state were to be called into question again). But can we be anti-Christian? In particular, can we profess and practice liberalism while denying or ignoring Christianity?

Liberals today tend to draw hasty conclusions on this point while contributing to the spreading of an anti-Christian attitude, so in order to find an answer, I suggest we turn to the founding fathers of their doctrine. It is an experience that requires intellectual effort, but it will be instructive and perhaps richly rewarding.

IN THE NAME OF THE FATHERS

In 1678, John Locke asked himself the following rhetorical question: "If he finds that God has made him and all other men in a state wherein they cannot subsist without society and has given them judgment to discern what is capable of preserving that society, can he but conclude he is obliged and that God requires him to follow those rules which conduce to the preservation of society?"[45] Over a hundred years later, Thomas Jefferson asked himself the same question (also posed in rhetorical form): "Can the liberties of a nation be thought secure when we have removed their only firm basis, a conviction in the minds of the people that these liberties are the gift of God? That they are not to be violated but with his wrath?"[46] Ten years later, in 1795, Kant raised the same issue: "In order to organize a group of rational beings who together require universal laws for their survival, but of whom each separate individual is secretly inclined to exempt himself from them, the constitution must be so designed that, although the citizens are opposed to one another in their private attitudes, these opposing views may inhibit one another in such a way that the public conduct of the citizens will be the same as if they did not have such evil attitudes."[47]

What did the great fathers mean by these interrogations, later to be echoed by other authoritative liberal voices?[48] They wished to establish three fundamental points of their liberal doctrine.

The first point: the problem. As Kant wrote, and as the fathers of the American Constitution reiterated, "The republican constitution is the only one which does complete justice to the rights of man but it is also the most difficult to establish, and even more so to preserve, so that many maintain that it would only be possible within a state of angels."[49] This is because it is threatened with disintegration. Indeed, as Locke said, men are "by nature all free, equal, and independent";[50] or as Jefferson phrased it in the Declaration of Independence, "all men are created equal, endowed by their creator with certain unalienable rights";[51] or in Kant's words, they enjoy "innate and inalienable rights, the necessary property of mankind."[52] Thus it is the effort of coexisting, or coexistence itself, that is the source of conflict, as Kant observed. "It suffices that they are there, that they surround him and that they are human beings, and they will mutually corrupt each other's moral disposition and make one another evil."[53] Hence the problem: "how could one expect to construct something completely straight from such crooked wood?"[54]

The second point: a condition. To eliminate or reduce this natural conflict, an equally natural law or irrefutable moral principle is needed. Locke wrote, "without this [natural] law, men can have no social intercourse or union among themselves."[55] Furthermore, "if you abolish the law of nature among them, you banish from among mankind at the same time the whole body politic, all authority, order, and fellowship among them."[56] Similarly, Kant held that the struggle every individual must make to overcome evil and to preserve order and social cohesion needs to take place "under the leadership of the good principle."[57]

Third point: the solution. This natural law and this good principle are directly dictated by the will of God or else derive from a specific imperative (an obligation) to create a society conforming to God's will. For Locke, "God, the author of this law, has willed it to be the rule of our moral life."[58] For Jefferson, as we have seen, the fundamental liberties must be regarded as "the gift of God." For Kant, we are bound by "a *duty* sui generis, not of human beings toward human beings but of the human race toward itself."[59]

How can we fulfill this duty? For Locke, we may do this by respecting the natural law, which is at once a (moral) divine law and a rational law. For Kant, "the dominion of the good principle is not otherwise attainable so far as human beings can work toward it than through the setting up and the diffusion of a society in accordance with, and for the sake of, the laws of virtue."[60] This society is the "ethical society," or the "juridico-civil society," the "ethical community," or an "ethical state (*ethischer Staat*), i.e., a kingdom of virtue (of the good principle)."[61] In short, it is a religious or religious-based state because "religion is (subjectively considered) the recognition of all our duties as divine commands."[62] Let us focus on this point.

Kant's point of departure, as we have noted, is the "problem of how it is to be arranged that in a society, however large, harmony in accordance with the principles of freedom and equality is maintained,"[63] or in other words, the construction of a liberal state in which the crooked wood of humanity may be partially made straight. His point of arrival is a political conception imbued with the Christian religion. In my interpretation, Kant's entire argument may be summed up as follows:

The ethical state is not imposed upon mankind by any mechanism of nature, even though "the highest task which nature has set for mankind must . . . be that of establishing . . . a perfectly just civil constitution,"[64] and even though "nature irresistibly wills that right should eventually gain the upper hand,"[65] because society is in any case subject to the power of evil.

The ethical state is not dictated only by the moral laws that can be drawn from the categorical imperative, because even though moral laws do indeed concern each individual, the state is more than a "distributive unity"[66] or a "disorderly mass." It is a "collective unity,"[67] a "moral personality,"[68] a "single whole" with a "common will."[69] Although a law of virtue is needed, it must be specific and appropriate: "in addition to prescribing laws to each individual human being, morally legislative reason also unfurls a banner of virtues as [a] rallying point for all those who love the good."[70]

Precisely because it must raise this banner of virtue, which is not a political banner, the ethical state cannot be governed by a political legislator. "Woe to the legislator who would want to bring about through coercion a polity directed to ethical ends!"[71]

Nor can the ethical state be self-governed. "If the community is to be an ethical one, the people, as a people, cannot itself be regarded as legislator."[72]

The conclusion follows by elimination. The ethical state is maintained by God, or more precisely by men who submit to God's will. "An ethical community is conceivable only as a people under divine commands, i.e. as a people of God, and indeed in accordance with the laws of virtue."[73]

Does this mean that the ethical state is not secular, that it must submit to another institution, to the church? *No.* In the (liberal) ethical state, men submit to their own (secular) reason, by which "the setting up and the diffusion of a society in accordance with, and for the sake of, the laws of virtue" are made to be "a task and duty" for them.[74] The separation of church and state is established.

Does this mean that in such a state the duty requiring us to submit to God's will pertains solely to the private sphere of the citizens? *No.* In the ethical (liberal) state, religion is so much a part of the public sphere that it is the very foundation of the state, and the guarantee of its subsistence. Religion is not a "comprehensive doctrine" for citizens to cultivate in private.

Does this mean that there is a God in the liberal state? *Yes—* the God of Christianity.

Does this mean that the reason of secularism is the reason of religion? *Yes.* Secular reason is Christian reason, because it transforms the commandments of the Gospel into rational imperatives.

On this point neither Kant nor the fathers of liberalism hesitated. For Kant, "although there are indeed different varieties of beliefs in divine revelation . . . there are not different religions. Of these forms, Christianity, as far as we know, is the most adequate."[75] For Jefferson, the moral system of Christianity is "the most perfect and sublime that has ever been taught by man,"[76] and "the Christian religion, when divested of the rags in which they have enveloped it and brought to the original purity and simplicity of its benevolent institutor, is a religion of all others most friendly to liberty, science, and the freest expansion of the human mind."[77] As for Locke, to understand his point of view we need only glance at the title of his last major work, *The Reasonableness of Christianity* (1695), in which he wrote, "where was there any such Code that Mankind might have recourse to, as their unerring Rule, before our Savior's time?"[78]

Locke was a sort of deist, as was Jefferson. Kant was a rationalist. All three reinterpreted or rewrote parts of the Bible. All three were liberals and also Christians. All three linked the fundamental rights of men and the foundation of the liberal state to the commandments of the Christian God. All three were "anticlerical" in their own ways, but none of them was "secular," "agnostic," a "nonbeliever," or an "atheist"—all categories they would not have understood or would have rejected.

These are not extrinsic, biographical facts, but essential points of liberal doctrine. Without *faith* in the equality, dignity, liberty, and responsibility of all men—that is to say, without a religion of man as the son and image of God (which is the essence of Judeo-Christian religion)—liberalism cannot defend the fundamental and universal rights of human beings or hope that human beings can coexist in a liberal society. A condition is necessary if liberals are to preserve the core of their doctrine. Basic human rights must be seen as a gift of God, to use Jefferson's phrase. They must be understood as the properties of men as human beings rather than as citizens, a possession not at the mercy of legislators but prior to their laws, and hence *pre*-political and *non*-negotiable. These rights must be *religiously* cherished.

Christianity and liberalism are *congeners*. If you remove faith in the former from the latter, then it too will disappear. Besides the historical evidence—that Europe became totalitarian when it abandoned Christianity for paganism, and that the United States has never known episodes of totalitarianism in its own history—there is also theoretical evidence.

In order to maintain a liberal society and a free-market society, which is one of its main components, a certain *ethos* and virtue are needed. Free institutions, free judges, and a free press are not enough. Even a free civil society is not enough. Principles and values must be respected within it, not as extrinsic, lawful obligations, but as personal and collective custom.[79] (This is why it is easy to export liberal institutions yet extremely arduous to build a liberal society.) Liberal freedom is not license, but "autonomy" (Kant); it is not egoism, but "well-intended interest" (Tocqueville). The liberal ethos derives from the idea that we are the children created in the image of the Christian God, who has given us truth and freedom, autonomy and the duty to fulfill His will. The list of liberal values is long and includes loyalty, honesty, credibility, tolerance, respect, justice, benevolence, etc., all those dispositions necessary to maintain an open, tolerant, and respectful society. These are typical Christian virtues that we find in scripture and the magisterium. If you take them away from liberalism, it loses its lifeblood.[80]

To sum up, both from a historical perspective and in accordance with the conceptual foundations of liberalism, the secular equation must be repudiated. The liberal *is* a Christian, even when he doesn't know it.

WHY LIBERALS SHOULD CALL THEMSELVES CHRISTIANS

Let us leave the fathers—with due thanks—and return to us. Liberalism today, as I have said, is so flawed that it is hard to speak of it as a single, coherent doctrine. Its theoretical crisis, even more than its political crisis, is so grave and strikes so deeply into its core that it is impossible to find remedy by readjusting outer, minor aspects. The main flaw of liberalism today is that it has retreated into a solely political and procedural dimension and has forgotten that it is also a *tradition*[81] with a rich, specific ethical content rooted in European and American history—a history of which Christianity is an essential part. Modernity has resisted and waged war against the church while feeding abundantly on its Christian heritage. Its very exaltation of the individual pays secular homage to the Christian message that man was created by God in order to discover the truth about himself and the world.

Anticlericalism explains why liberals have forgotten this symbiosis, but it cannot justify their forgetfulness. If we want to save liberalism and preserve liberal regimes, we cannot use contingent historical facts as the constitutional basis of a doctrine. We cannot allow the "Roman question" to compromise the "Christian question," because these two issues are not necessarily connected. Those who promote the former in order to elude the latter are neither secular nor liberal, but rather are unaware of the pitfalls of liberalism and are insensitive both politically and morally. Liberals must know that just as the "healthy secularism" described by Benedict XVI is not antireligious, so "healthy liberalism" is not anti-Christian. The opposite is true.

A decalogue of reasons may help us understand why liberals should call themselves Christian. They should—

1) If they remember their origins. The entire liberal movement originated with a sort of "Copernican" idea, a radical overturning of the old hierarchies. The liberty of man springs from the truth that he is made in the image of God, who has placed him at the center of the world. God created man in His image, gave him dignity as a human being, and endowed him

with reason so that he would be responsible for his actions. God made him brother to every other human being in the unique community of mankind. This idea is clearly Christian, or rather Judeo-Christian. "The truth shall set you free." (John 8:32; Galatians 5:1) *The* truth, not the sum of diverse, partial, and powerless truths.

2) If they are aware of the dangers faced by their doctrine and the crisis of their society today. The liberal society is not just any aggregate—open, indistinct, and indifferent. It is a moral and spiritual unity that requires adequate customs and appropriate virtues. Without the Christian idea that we are a people of God, knowing no historical, geographical, or cultural boundaries, and that we are commanded to fulfill His will by cultivating certain personal and social virtues on this earth, the liberal doctrine would be nothing more than a hopeless aspiration. Liberal cosmopolitanism is related to Christian ecumenism, to the idea of the unity (rational and moral) of all mankind.

3) If they realize that liberalism cannot be "self-sufficient." As we can see when controversy touches principles, the foundations of science are not scientific and the foundations of politics are not political. In the end, what is needed is a choice, an option, a decision. The decision to found a liberal state (and a democratic one, insofar as this is compatible) in which everyone is free and equal, despite contrary evidence, means choosing responsibility for oneself and goodwill toward one's fellow human beings. It is a Christian decision.

4) If they wish to solve the problem of political loyalty and social stability. In order not to destroy society by deteriorating into license and violence, individual freedom requires limits: a sense of sinfulness, of what is forbidden, unthinkable, nonnegotiable. This limit cannot be established only by positive law, at whatever level (constitutional, international, etc.), because such

a law could always be overridden. A moral, religious limit is needed, or one that is experienced as religious. The Christian limit is not putting oneself in God's place but respecting His will, or not arousing the "wrath of God," about which Jefferson spoke.

5) If they do not wish to become ethnocentric, and to reduce their regimes to mere fortunate tribes and human rights to the privileges of a few cultures. Liberalism has universal aspirations. The rights of human beings are to liberals as the laws of nature are to scientists: once discovered (not invented) by someone at a certain time and place, they are valid for all and forever. But just as the laws of nature refer to an order inscribed in the world, the rights of human beings refer to a God who has stamped His image upon man. And this is clearly the Christian vision of God, creator of the natural and moral world.

6) If they wish to give a conceptual and not just an aggressive historical basis to the separation of church and state. Christianity justifies the separation between throne and altar as a matter of principle, not one of convenience. From the Christian point of view, man submits to his Creator, who endows him with moral liberty and dignity. He also submits to the state that grants him political freedom and citizenship. The great division between Caesar and God is first and foremost a division of principles rather than one of institutions. Historically, the issue has been subject to tormented debate and has taken centuries to work through, but conceptually it is very simple and linear. Liberals have won a battle against the church, but they have had Christianity as their ally.

7) If they wish to prevent dire prophecies regarding their political regimes from coming true, such as Plato's prophecy "is not the avidity of democracy for that which is its definition and criterion of good [and that is liberty] the thing which dissolves it

too?" *Republic*, VIII, 562b), or that of John Paul II, "a democracy without values easily turns into open or thinly disguised totalitarianism."[82] Freedom can destroy itself. Who or what can keep a free society in check if, as Jefferson noted, those liberties are not cherished as "the gift of God"? Liberals, who thanks to their fathers' efforts have founded their own doctrine on this gift, should know better than anyone else that it can save their society from the risks of self-destruction.

8) If they preserve the atrocious memory of what happened in Europe when, rather than "unfurl the banner" of Christianity as Kant urged them to do, Europeans became pagans and tore themselves apart with civil and religious wars and clashes of civilizations, bloodying their own lands and sinking into the abjection of concentration camps. Many have asked, "Where was God at the time of Auschwitz?" They ought to finish the question with "And why did the liberals abandon Him?"

9) If they wish to solve the moral crisis of Europe and of the West. Our civilization is being destroyed by an overt crisis of faith, by a loss of belief in religious values, especially in the values of the European tradition. The apostasy of Christianity is eroding our identity because it keeps us from recognizing the heritage we share and from feeling a sense of mutual belonging. Today, Europe is a well-stocked market regulated by treaties of reciprocal benefit, where goods are exchanged but values are sold cheap, where we are free because we are diverse, but also where we are diverse because we are strangers to each other. If the liberal leaders of Europe do not recover its identity, if they refuse to raise the banner of their heritage, then the entire process of European unification will splinter into nationalities, particularities, ethnic groups, egoisms.

10) Finally, liberals should call themselves Christians if they want to preserve their pride in their civilization, support it under

challenge, assist it in difficulty, and defend it from attack. Our civilization sprang into being at the foot of the Cross, and under that sign it divided into factions and fought its battles inside and outside its territory. It hardly knows how to exist without the Cross. Like Christians, liberals admit to no geographical boundaries, because, as is written in the Letter to Diognetus, "They do not distinguish themselves from other men, neither for land, language, clothing."[83] Nor do they accept any social barriers, because, as St. Paul wrote in the Epistle to the Galatians, "There is neither Jew nor Greek, nor slave nor freeman, nor man nor woman, because you are one in Jesus Christ."[84] This cosmopolitanism is the sign of a mission. Just as the Christian carries his faith in the Son of God throughout the world, the liberal promotes his faith in the basic freedoms of human beings and exports it all over the globe. Caution may slow him down at times, but not the concept by which he is stirred to action.

SHOULD WE CALL OR CAN WE HELP CALLING OURSELVES CHRISTIANS?

Two questions must be answered. First: to be liberal, should we call ourselves Christians, or is it enough to say that we cannot help calling ourselves Christians? Second: if Christianity is the foundation and food of liberalism, then should liberals be believers, and should the liberal state be religious rather than secular?

"Why We Cannot Help Calling Ourselves Christians" is the well-known title of an essay by Benedetto Croce. A splendid essay—lucid, vigorous, serene—composed between "hopes and fears"[85] in 1942, it belongs to the literature on the crisis of European civilization that views the aftermath of "the two great religious wars," the First and Second World Wars, as a descent into hell for Europe, for liberalism, and for Christianity.

For Croce, "Christianity was the greatest revolution that the human race has ever accomplished," and "no other revolutions will bear comparison with this." Further, "the revolutions and discoveries which have followed in modern times . . . can only be conceived as dependent upon the Christian revolution."[86] *All of them.* A polemic against Christianity or against the institution of the church is "as unreasonable as one against the universities or other places of learning,"[87] because Christianity is at work in the "humanists of the Renaissance," in the "great reformers," in the "austere founders of physico-mathematical science," in the "preachers of natural religion and of natural rights and of tolerance," in the "reasoners of the Age of Enlightenment," in the "revolutionaries who spread their achievement from France all over Europe," in the "philosophers who directly or indirectly succeeded in giving critical and speculative range to the idea of the Spirit."[88] In other words, as Croce wrote elsewhere, "modern civilization and thought are Christian and are the continuation of the impulse given by Jesus and Paul."[89] There is "a connection between the message of Jesus and the life of liberty," and "Christianity lies at the bottom of modern thought and its ethical ideal,"[90] so we may say that "liberalism is essentially Christian."[91]

Why then should we limit ourselves to the assertion: "We cannot help calling ourselves Christians"? Why not conclude instead that "We should or must call ourselves Christians?" What is the difference between these two statements? Although this is not the place for a technical discussion of Croce's philosophical system, it is his particular brand of liberalism, stemming not from the fathers but from Hegel, that we must call into question. It is a theoretically more robust source of the secular equation. If many liberals have accepted this equation and have neglected or rejected Christianity, it is due in part to the influence of Benedetto Croce and idealism.

For Croce, liberalism is not a social, economic, or political movement. It is not a doctrine, a philosophy, a system of thought, an agenda, or a political party even when a few liberals band together to form a party. It is a "total conception of the world and of reality,"[92] a "metapolitical conception."[93] This conception is characterized by liberty (in the singular), which is an "idea," and not by the juridical-political liberties (in the plural), which are only "ephemeral institutions"[94] that strive to give substance to the former. As an idea, liberty is the Spirit in history; it is the rational in the real. The "unfolding of the Spirit" (or rather the "dialectic of the Spirit," a crucial expression in Croce's system) is itself the path to freedom. Since the Spirit must unfold and since the Spirit is liberty, it can be hindered, blocked, and even suspended due to "illness," "growing crises," "accidents"[95] (in the form of a "parenthesis" such as fascism), but it is always at work.

Here a problem arises. How may we reconcile this immanentistic conception of the Spirit (and of liberalism) with the Christian revolution? Where precisely should this revolution be located? Is it "a historical process, with its place in the general historical process as the most fateful of all its crises,"[96] so that in the future course of history "no man can tell if another religious revelation . . . will come to pass for the human race?"[97] Or is it a "moment" of the Spirit unfolding through history so that "the Christian God is still our God, and the philosophies to which we owe allegiance call him Spirit, which is always beyond us and yet always our very selves"?[98]

Depending on what road we choose, the link between Christianity and liberalism changes. On one hand, if Christianity stands to the Spirit as *ought to be* stands to *is*, then the universal ethical value of Christianity is safe, but the immanence of liberty in history is lost, because what *ought to be* remains beyond what *is*, and always will. On the other hand, if Christianity is the Spirit itself or one of its "moments," then the immanence of liberty in the historical process is safe, but the specific nature of the Christian revolution is lost. This is because a revolution has a fixed date of birth, but the Spirit, precisely because it is always unfolding through history, cannot have a historical beginning. According to the former interpretation (Christianity as a transcendent element of ethical comparison), Croce's essay is one of the highest praises of Christianity. Seen as a revolution, Christianity is the baptismal act of our civilization, the source of law, morals, the modern state, and liberalism. According to the latter interpretation (Christianity as a "moment" of the Spirit's unfolding in history), Croce's essay becomes one of the crudest declarations of the death of Christianity. Seen as a historical accident or a phase of the Spirit, Christianity loses its transcendent dimension. On one hand, it presents itself as a "miracle" or "mystery" that men can embrace as an anchor to save themselves from the crisis of our civilization; on the other hand, it "was no miracle invading the course of history"[99] and "we no longer worship it as a mystery."[100] In one sense, the idealist philosopher is a secular Christian; in the other, "there is a sharp contrast between the idealist philosopher and the religious man."[101]

Croce was unable to decide which road to take without putting his whole system at stake. He divided himself: Croce the politician and historiographer, who felt anguished by the crisis of Europe, chose the Christian revolution. Croce the philosopher, who contemplated history as the unfolding of liberty, chose the immanence of the Spirit in which this revolution is absorbed. "If the religious man cannot help but see the philosopher as his adversary, or even as his mortal enemy, the latter sees in the former a younger brother, his own self at a previous moment."[102]

This explains the formula "Why we cannot help calling ourselves Christians." In its ambivalence, this formula expresses the only compatible link between Christianity and idealistic philosophy. The price of that compatibility is that the former must become the childhood of the Spirit, which will look upon it as mystery revealed.

Clearly, Croce's formula would have displeased the fathers. Can a doctrine of liberty be liberal if indeed liberty is not held to be a victory, a basic right, a value, "a gift of God," but rather an attribute of the absolute Spirit that can never be lost, that never contracts or disappears, whatever be the fate of individuals and peoples? Can a conception of liberty be called "liberal" if, as Croce maintains, it may be combined even with a collectivist economic order or an authoritarian political regime?

Croce's formula that liberty and Spirit are the same thing offers a philosophical justification for the secular equation. The Spirit unfolding in history is a secular spirit because it is prior to and independent from the Christian Holy Spirit. We call it Spirit or even Providence, but it is not the Christian Providence or Spirit. We may invoke the latter and it will assist us; to the other we cannot pray. When we stumble it cannot see the vale of tears into which we fall, because for it there are neither vales nor falls, only the serene plain of the eternal unfolding of Spirit—History—Liberty. The same holds true for Croce's "religion of liberty." This religion has no place of worship, symbols, or scriptures; it has no saints, prophets, or martyrs.

Its script is vague and its actors are acted upon rather than protagonists. Thus Croce's liberalism and that of the Hegelian school is not secular by accident, by reaction to the church, or because of its author's personal lack of faith, for indeed, as he himself wrote, his faith was strong: "I am more Christian than most people who profess themselves as such, to say nothing of the opportunism of neo-converts."[103] His brand of liberalism is secular by necessity because of its inner philosophical substance. It is a liberalism that prizes Christianity, speaks of it with reverence and deep emotion, and views it as the motor of civilization and the shaping force of the European Spirit, yet could not decide to embrace it. This is why "We cannot help calling ourselves Christians," not because Christianity is the religious and moral foundation of our liberties, but because the Spirit absorbs it.

The liberalism of the fathers was not like that. Believers or nonbelievers, practicing or not, they held that we should call ourselves Christians because liberalism is based on an ethical and Christian religious view. It was not the Spirit but the Christian God that endowed us with our liberties.

AS IF GOD EXISTED

We have come to the final question: If liberals should call themselves Christians, then should they also be believers? And if so, does this mean that the liberal state is not secular?

Let us tackle the latter question first. For practical and political purposes, we may provide a definition of the secular state in negative terms: it is not theocratic; it neither submits to any church nor makes decisions based on religious texts. However, in positive terms, it is hard to formulate a clear and exhaustive definition as to what it is. An aura of ambiguity and uncertainty remains even if we have recourse to institutional terms. The separation of church and state is all very well, but the familiar formula of "a free church in a free state" has different meanings in different countries. In Italy, for example, it once signified depriving the pope of temporal power while leaving him free to preach in his role as pope, whereas today it means forbidding the pope to intervene in questions concerning our society. The American equivalent of this formula, the "wall of separation" as Jefferson defined it, means something quite different: protecting religion and the natural rights of man from the interference of the state, rather than the other way around.[104]

We can say that secular states make their decisions on the basis of their leaders' *free convictions*. But we cannot require those convictions to be "rational," if indeed that term has any meaning, to the exclusion of all else. Is it rational to decide on the basis of a biased interest—of category, of power, and not, may I ask, on the basis of our forefathers' faith? We cannot demand that free convictions be divorced from religious ones. When someone has been called upon to make an important decision, how can we ask him to set aside part of himself and to silence what he most reveres and believes in? Nor can we demand that the discussion of religion in public discourse be conditioned by "provisos" such as those suggested by Rawls and Habermas: How can a liberal obstruct debate between free persons? So, once the secular state has decreed that its decisions are to be made by its legitimate representatives, no limits can be established for their debate other than the rules of courtesy, tolerance, reasonableness, and respect for the law. The only principle regulating public discourse is that *debate must be free*, and the only limit is *you cannot suppress debate*.[105] To ask for more, to willfully regiment public discourse by excluding religion is impossible, or, as is obvious in so many secular arguments, it is only a surreptitious way of imposing the motives of certain groups for certain aims and not those of others.

The first question is much more serious: If the liberal should be a Christian, should he also be a believer? *Yes* and *no*.

The word "Christian believer" has two meanings, just as "secular" does. First, it refers to those who believe in the God made flesh, the God of the Revelation, Crucifixion, and Resurrection. Second, it refers to those who believe in the teachings and the message of that God. We may distinguish between them by calling the former "Christians by faith," and the latter "Christians by culture," or followers of Christ and admirers of the Christian message, or more simply the faithful and the secular. They are different from each other, but they both *believe*. Technically speaking, they both profess a *faith*.

The believer in Christ is someone who has had a direct, personal experience of Him. The believer speaks to Christ and He answers. The believer loves Christ and He loves him in return. The believer suffers and Christ comforts him. The believer in Christ believes in the Person of Jesus and has faith in that Person.

The admirer of the Christian message is someone who believes that Christianity has changed the world, that it has brought about an unprecedented moral revolution of love, equality, and dignity, whose effects are still at work today. He believes that had this revolution never occurred, the world would be a far worse place; the life of man would be more savage, basic human rights without sufficient guarantee, and our prospects less hopeful. He also believes that the culture of Christianity is of great value to himself and to others; that it is a good unto itself.

Both believers have received a gift. For the believer in Christ, that "gift of God" is grace, the unasked for, mysterious experience of an encounter with Him. For the believer in Christian culture, the "gift of God" is our Christian heritage of virtues, customs, habits, institutions—in short, our civilization.

It is not necessary that liberals be Christians in the former sense; whether they are or not, this concerns their personal life, a realm unfathomable to others and beyond their criticism. It is essential that they be Christians in the latter sense, because being Christian by culture means possessing a foundation for our doctrine, a guide for our actions, a reference point, and a sign of hope.

But all that is still not enough. Those who stop at *believing that* must not hold back from *believing in*. We must go beyond the rationalism that confines us to our calculations, beyond the positivism that binds us to the testimony of our senses, beyond the scientism that accepts only experimental proof. We must not allow our yearning for the divine and the sacred, our experience of mystery and the infinite to be purged from our inner life. We cannot be whole human beings without these dimensions. And we cannot be liberals of only one dimension.

Can we take the leap between *believing that* and *believing in*? Yes, it can be done, because nothing keeps us from doing so. Then can we be asked to take that leap? No one can ask this of us, because faith cannot be proved or imposed. But would it be useful for us to take this leap?

With his famous wager, Pascal answered in the affirmative. Kant followed in his footsteps with his independent argument: Morality is impossible without God, therefore, "It is morally necessary to assume the existence of God,"[106] or "it is morally certain that there is a God." In one word, we must live *velut si Deus daretur,* as if God existed.

Does this maxim hold true for us today?[107] Does it hold true for liberals? It *must* hold true. To live as if God existed means to deny man that giddy feeling of omnipotence and absolute freedom which at first elates him and then depresses and degrades him. It means recognizing our finite condition and becoming aware of the ethical limitations of our actions. This amounts to establishing our rights and acknowledging our duties.

"It is only with religion that the hope of happiness first arises," Kant wrote.[108] It is not only our happiness that needs religion. Without the Christian vision of the human person, our political life is doomed to become the mere exercise of power and our science to divorce itself from moral wisdom; our technology to become indifferent to ethics and our material well-being blind to our exploitation of others and our environment. Without that vision, our encounter with "the other"—the poor, the sick, the dying, the needy or outcast of any gender, race, or age—can only deteriorate into violence and manipulation, and our civilization will cut itself off from the principles that first baptized and nurtured it. Yes, *velut si Deus daretur* is the moral condition necessary in order for us to cultivate hope.

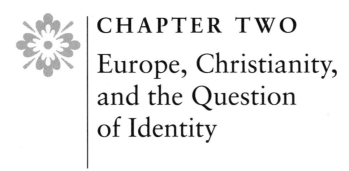

CHAPTER TWO

Europe, Christianity, and the Question of Identity

WHAT IS EUROPE?

In the previous chapter, I argued that the crisis of liberalism today stems from its refusal to recognize itself as an intellectual tradition springing from the Christian ethic. I also suggested that the current moral crisis of Europe and the West is due to an apostasy of Christianity. Here I intend to connect the two issues, using Europe as a case study. The thesis that I will be defending is that the constant delays and failures in the political unification of Europe owe largely to its refusal to recognize its own Christian identity. Put differently, if first I tried to prove that liberals should call themselves Christians, here I will try to prove that Europe should define itself as Christian if it truly desires unification. We may cast this thesis in general and negative terms. If we view liberalism solely as a political and not also as a metaphysical doctrine, if we do not see it as being rooted in the Christian ethic that is characteristic of the liberal Western states, sedimented in their history and enshrined in their charters, then those states are destined to lose their identity. If they lose their identity, they will also lose their cohesion. The apostasy of Christianity is exposing the entire West to the risk of a grave cultural and political crisis, and perhaps even to a collapse of civilization.

But let's return to Europe, our case study. My argument is as follows: First, the unification of Europe requires that we define European identity. Second, the European identity proposed by liberal culture today is paradoxical because it is not specifically *European*. Third, the attempt to resolve this paradox through the typically liberal solution of constitutional patriotism cannot solve the problem of unification because it produces an ethical deficit. Fourth, this ethical deficit derives from the refusal of liberals to baptize Europe in the waters of Christian values. Finally, since Europe cannot be unified unless it first claims an identity of its own, it follows that the liberal doctrine as understood and practiced today is an obstacle to its unification. If Europe truly desires unification, then it should call itself Christian.

Before going on to my thought experiment, let's see where Europe stands today in the process of unification. It is a long and tedious story, full of twists and turns. To liven it up, I will use a literary device previously employed by Montesquieu in his *Persian Letters* with the intent of uniting "philosophy, politics, and ethics" in a single novel.[1] Montesquieu imagined a caravan of Persians traveling far and wide, observing European customs and institutions. With no claims to such literary skill, I will imagine an American traveler, Johnny, writing his *American Letters* to his girlfriend, Danielle, with the main purpose of understanding if Europe is about to witness the birth of a nation or something approaching it. An American is the right sort of person for such an undertaking, first because Americans get straight to the point, and second, being strongly patriotic, they are capable of grasping the essence of the problem at hand.

Most likely Johnny will entertain Danielle as his predecessor Usbek amused Roxane, his beloved (at least until the fatal day she betrayed him), by describing to her the "wonderful and strange customs" of the Europeans.[2] Often he will find himself repeating Usbek's very words, which just proves that although time passes quickly in Europe, it leaves an indelible trace. For example, indulging his puritanism a bit, he will write: "Women here have lost all sense of decorum; they appear before men with their faces uncovered as if courting their own defeat. They encourage them with their glances; they see them in the mosques, when they take walks, and in their own homes."[3] Moreover, "it is hard to believe how much it costs a man to keep his wife in fashion."[4] Furthermore, "I have not observed in Christians the intense belief in their religion that is apparent in Muslims; for Christians there is a great distance from profession to belief, from belief to conviction, from conviction to practice."[5] He will tell Danielle that in Europe, by contrast with America, the powerful "are in a different situation: disgrace deprives them of nothing but goodwill and favor; they retire from court and expect to enjoy a peaceful life and the advantages of their birth."[6] He will note that here, "law as it stands today is a science that teaches princes how far they may contravene justice without running counter to their interests."[7] He will observe that "Paris is the seat of the government of the empire of Europe,"[8] and that "the most powerful states of Europe are those belonging to the emperor and to the kings of France, Spain, and England," while the princes of Italy, with their small, disunited realms, are "the most to be pitied," because "their states are as open as caravan-serais, to which they are forced to welcome all comers."[9]

Coming to his and our main topic of interest, Johnny will see in Europe the signs of uniformity and unity that would seem to indicate a homogeneous society sharing many goals and significant aspects, ranging from cultural symbols to economics, institutions to legislation, customs to religion. The following passages drawn from Johnny's letters, collected in chapters, contain his most important observations and impressions in this regard.

* * *

Symbols

"Dear Dany—the first thing I noticed when I got to Brussels is that Europe has its own flag, always flown alongside the local one. The flag of Europe has a circle of twelve stars on a dark blue background, which stand for the states belonging to the union when the flag was first hoisted and unfurled. Although the number of member states continues to increase (at the present time, there are 27, with several more lined up to join), they won't be adding any more new stars to the flag. This isn't because they want to give special emphasis or priority to those first twelve members, but because the twelve stars are related to an image of the Apocalypse from which the flag's designer drew inspiration. I also listened to the European anthem, the melody of which was borrowed from the 'Ode to Joy' of Beethoven's *Ninth Symphony*, but without the words. (I suspect that Schiller's verses, *Bruder, uberm Sternenzelt/Muss ein lieber Vater wohnen*, 'Brothers, above the starry sky dwells a loving father,' were not secular enough.) No one puts their hand on their heart the way we do whenever the anthem is played, so it is a bit like listening to an uplifting, familiar tune that puts you in a good mood. The European anthem is associated with a motto, 'United in Diversity' or 'Unity in Diversity,' which is recited for special occasions, such as May 5th, the 'birthday' of the European Union, commemorating a declaration made by Robert Schuman, a sort of saintly, Catholic Thomas Jefferson, who, however, is completely unknown to ordinary people in Europe. Europe even has a patron saint, St. Benedict, recommended by Pope Paul VI. At first glance, Europeans seem united, but this is merely an impression. Now I'll move on to something else and tell you about the social life of Europeans."

European Lifestyles

"Dear Dany—I am writing you from Paris, but it might be from anywhere else in Europe. Europeans all do the same things and have similar lifestyles. At the supermarket, they all buy the same products: the same tomatoes, all perfectly round, ripe, and tasteless (like ours); the same pears (all hard as rocks); and the same cucumbers (all exactly the same size and shape). At my own expense, I have learned that these products are exactly identical wherever you go because, I have been told, nothing really tasty, not even the tiniest morsel of sharp cheese, spicy ham, or creamy mozzarella, is allowed to slip by the European Union bureau that is responsible for deadening taste buds and exterminating flavor. It's no wonder that Europeans crave fast food like hamburgers and French fries. On TV they all watch the same programs, just like ours: talk shows, musicals, and soap operas, or programs like *Big Brother, Who Wants to Be a Millionaire,* and the *Eurovision Song Contest.* At the stadium, I watched the European football championship games of the UEFA Champions League and the Europa League. At the movie theaters, wherever you go, they show Hollywood films and you can consume as much popcorn and Coke as you like. Students can move from one university to another, like they do in America, and now there are a few European universities too. Only the churches are different, much older and more beautiful than ours—but in general, religious services are usually deserted except for a few old ladies. Sometimes the mass is shouted out and sung so raucously you'd think you were at a pop concert or a rodeo. Luckily, they tell me, Pope Benedict XVI has reintroduced the use of Latin for the mass, so maybe it will become more solemn and mystic again. Bye for now, I'm on my way to Frankfurt."

The Economy

"My dear Dany—Viewed from this flourishing financial center, the European economy seems solid enough, although some people are puzzled by it, given these times of crisis. For example, European bankers are especially proud of something that troubles European leaders: the euro, which has crushed our greenback while sending some people halfway to the poorhouse. It's very strange, though, because the euro comes only in large bills, but almost nobody here will accept the largest bill as payment, and as for the smallest, it is practically worthless, while our one-dollar bill can still buy you something to eat. The pictures on the bills are all of imaginary bridges, towers, Gothic windows, Renaissance portals, and abstract designs. I asked around to find out why they didn't put portraits of the great European geniuses on their paper money and was told that they didn't want to depict illustrious Italians, Frenchmen, or Germans for fear of hurting the feelings of the smaller countries without such rich cultural traditions. But there is a single European Central Bank, which doesn't have to answer to anyone. And there are single markets of goods, capital, services, and workers that all operate in regimes of protected and controlled liberty, which here is called 'social economy of the market,' or also, in the UK, 'the third way,' as if to suggest that Europeans stand midway between our American capitalism and the communism of the ex-Soviet countries. My next letter will be from Rome, the best setting for my next topic."

Human Rights

"Dany Darling—Here in this Wonderland I have seen something fantastic: the triumph of human rights. Believe me, of all the places in the world, Europe is where human rights are most protected and guaranteed. As far as political rights go, nobody is excluded, and there's a little something for everybody: passersby, guests, immigrants, and illegal aliens, to such an extent they are talking of giving them *all* the right to vote. As far as civil rights go, they now have so many they don't know how to make up any more. Civil rights here are like new makes of automobiles; and maybe that's why they often talk about rights of 'the newest make.' Human rights are a specialty of the place and are in rapid expansion so that they have even been extended to monkeys, which must not be allowed to live in 'bestial' or 'inhumane' conditions. As far as social rights are concerned, Europe is overwhelmed by them. Every imaginable request from workers is granted through new legislation: maternity and paternity leave, safety standards for hazardous work conditions, retirement pensions for people of all ages, super-short workweeks, time off for just about any saint's day or strike or other occasion, unemployment benefits, underoccupation benefits, laziness benefits—you name it! Europe has the most generous welfare setup of any place on earth. And yet, people complain all the time, even though it's not like home. Here in Europe everyone wants more state intervention, not less. Frankly, I can't understand them. Doesn't more state intervention mean less freedom? More later. Love."

The Church

"Dear Dany—Since I am in the Eternal City, I'm going to tell you about the church. I'll be brief, because the topic is so huge. You know what I think: I am very fond of our American model, the 'wall of separation' that our forefathers built *not* in order to protect the state, as everybody here seems to think, but to safeguard religious freedom. In Europe, it's very different. As the church has found itself so often siding against the birth of nation-states, and as it has had to seek out a modus vivendi for itself, here concordats are the rule. There is no doubt that the church benefits from this situation, but it would seem to put the spiritual authority of its teachings at a disadvantage. If you allow yourself to be financed by the state, thereby obtaining advantages and privileges, then you have to pay the price, which means sometimes you may have to hold your tongue. One example of this is when they were drafting the European Constitution. A great pope, John Paul II, with his celebrated apostolic exhortation of 2003, *Ecclesia in Europa,* thundered against the exclusion from the Constitution of any reference to Christianity as the great taproot of Europe, but then everything was settled without much further protest from the church by granting protection to the national concordats. Europe did not wish to recognize itself as Christian, but was willing to concede a protected status to Christian institutions.

"Another thing that doesn't convince me is this: as you know, here in Europe everything is becoming more and more secularized, so many people have lost their faith, or don't practice their religion, or no longer feel a religious vocation. The church doesn't seem to realize that much of this secularization is the result of the welfare state and of the concept of social justice, to which its own social doctrine also appeals. So I wonder, if the state gives you everything that your family, your parish, and your community once gave you, why do you even need a church? If people are handed over to the care of the state or a public entity from the moment they are born, why shouldn't they grow up secularized, without a religion, or even against religion?

"Then there is the question of Islam. Here the word 'dialogue' is much in vogue. That's all right up to a point in speaking of politics, but not of religion. People here are pretty upset. If we are invaded or attacked, what are we supposed to do, turn the other cheek? Why is the church on the frontlines when it comes to defending Muslims' right to build mosques, but so cautious when it comes to demanding the reciprocity evoked by John Paul II in his exhortation of 2003? Why does it welcome immigration from Islamic countries with open arms?

"To be frank, my impression is that after the Second Vatican Council, the church has begun to flirt a bit with modernity. This is a mistake because it is leading the church down the path of politics, and dividing it just as the political world is divided into 'conservatives' and 'progressivists.' As a result, it risks being discredited exactly as party politics has been discredited. Is it any wonder that people swarm around Benedict XVI as they did around John Paul II, while the churches continue to stand empty?"

Institutions

"Dany—Today I will tell you about European institutions. What a mess! First, Europe has a Parliament to which every five years Europeans entrust a few powers, even though they don't really know what powers the Parliament has, or they couldn't care less, or they don't trust it at all. Most people will tell you that it's very expensive to maintain this Parliament that sits both in Brussels and in Strasbourg, and that its only function is to serve as a forum to discuss the fate of the universe, recommend new rights, and penalize countries that haven't aligned themselves with all its standards (usually Italy, and on one occasion Austria). Next, Europe also has a Commission, which serves as a government, but its members are nominated by the national governments. It has so many commissioners who do so many things, and they usually have it in for us Americans because they claim we won't let them do things right. There is a European Council, which is made up of European ministers who set guidelines and generally manage things. There is a Court of Justice, which settles litigation among member states. There is a Court of Human Rights, which sees that people's rights are respected: both those rights already stipulated and the new ones they make up as they go along, sort of like what our Supreme Court ought to do according to some liberals. There is a 'common juridical space,' which means that you can be arrested and charged in one country by a policeman or magistrate of another country, even for something that may be against the law in the former country but not in the latter. There is a single 'space of transit' in which every European may circulate freely without a passport, but inexplicably many non-EU citizens also manage to enjoy this privilege (and among them are many jobless and homeless people as well as criminals). There is a Charter of Fundamental Rights, which spells out the basic rights and duties of European citizens. There is a tangled mass of common laws called the *acquis communautaire* in the jargon of Brussels, a compendium of over 90,000 pages containing all the norms that regulate various aspects of life for all the citizens of the European Union. Finally, there was also a Constitution, which however was rejected by referendum in France and the Netherlands in 2005, then rewritten in an even more incomprehensible text and rejected by a third referendum in Ireland in 2008. So it is no longer valid, because in Europe all decisions must be unanimous or else they are not binding. Recently the Constitution has been replaced by a treaty signed in Lisbon. So what do you think about that? Bye."

The Union

"Dear Dany—This is the last letter that I will be writing to you before we meet in Dallas. You ask me now to draw my conclusions. Is there a United Europe? Frankly, you put me on the spot. Despite all the unified, united, coordinated, and identical things I have seen over here, my answer is no. First, Europe has no legitimately democratic political institutions. I mean there is no true state or super-state. Not even the European Parliament is an arena of democratic political struggle, because it counts so little or not at all. How can Europeans believe that they are citizens of Europe? Nobody knows what the European government really is, to whom it must answer, what powers it has, or what its limits are. It isn't clear if the Commission decides or simply executes. Everything seems to be in the hands of the national ministers and leaders who, meeting in special summits behind closed doors in Brussels or some other pleasant but unknown spot of Europe (had you ever heard of Laeken or Maastricht before?), make decisions that they don't have the power or the courage to make at home.

"Yes, it's true that Europeans have juridical citizenship that grants them special rights, in particular the right to free movement within Europe, which they take advantage of, though at times circumspectly. Once when a couple of Poles threatened to migrate, there was an immediate outbreak of the "Polish plumber syndrome," to which the European Union replied with a directive that hushed the matter up. But you see, Europeans don't yet have real political citizenship. Moreover, as becomes clear if we observe its behavior in any serious international crisis, Europe is not a geopolitical subject with its own international policies. It is weak. It doesn't want to spend money on defense or keep its own army. It adopts a strategy of appeasement in dealing with dictators, or when menaced by terrorism or by threats to shut down its gas pipelines. It speaks with a chorus of tongues, at times in unison, at other times discordantly, and always exclusively with the goal of 'dialogue,' 'peace,' 'multilateralism,' in order to function as a counterweight to America. You know, Europeans really had it in for Bush, as they had it in for Reagan before that. Finally, from an economic point of view, Europe does not have a plan for integration. There are many major sectors that member states have no intention of unifying.

"To sum up, dear Dany, Europe, as those who know it best all agree, is a truly unique creature. Many praise it to the skies. Some people even claim that Europe will be the leader of the twenty-first century: 'The European Union is starting to develop an enormous sphere of influence, extending way beyond its borders, that could be called 'the Eurosphere,'' and which will soon surpass America.[10] There are others who consider it a super-state, saying that 'It is this key legal supremacy of the EU over the fifteen nation-states that is the very heart of the case that the EU is already a state.'[11] There are those who speak of a 'United States of Europe,' which will soon cause 'a geopolitical earthquake . . . that will have a profound effect on the world of the twenty-first century and America's place in it.'[12] And some people, even more enthusiastically, speak of a 'European dream' that will eclipse our American dream.[13] On the other hand, the European Union has many detractors. According to some, the process of European unification is the 'most spectacular *coup d'état* in history,' or nothing more than a conspiracy to promote 'the power, wealth, influence and glory of France.'[14] Others agree, describing the Union as a 'sphere of French hegemony'[15] or a 'French design' with which 'Germany has co-operated' and to which it has 'acquiesced.'[16] Some speak of 'EUtopia'[17] or of 'EUrabia.'[18] Others believe it has written the 'epitaph for an old continent.'[19] Still others lament its impotence[20] or easy compliance,[21] its loss of Christian roots[22] or its population decrease. The literature on the subject is endless.

"To conclude, honey, what can I say? Even the closest circle of member-friends who make up an exclusive and lofty club are down in the dumps these days. The Union, they admit, simply does not exist, and I agree. Europe today is like a ghost materializing before your eyes wherever you look, but when you try to pin it down, you can find no trace of it. It is powerful yet feeble. Rich but noncompetitive. Strong-willed but dreadfully shy. Robustly built but peace-loving. Neither intergovernmental nor communal, it is simply in between. This is why I am convinced that as a political and institutional reality European unity simply does not exist. I'm not the only one who says so.

Many European experts, as well as most citizens, think so and complain about the situation.[23] See you soon."

* * *

We'll stop here. Is Johnny right? I think he is more right than wrong. Accents, irony, and idiosyncrasies apart, Europe today resembles the picture sketched in these not so fictitious *American Letters*. Why?

THE PROBLEM OF THE SOUL

At the beginning of the 1990s, when economic unification became more stringent and political unification became a major goal, many politicians raised a vital issue: in order to become one single nation or one single state, Europe needed a *soul*. In a speech given on February 4, 1992, Jacques Delors, then president of the European Commission, asserted, "We must give Europe a soul. . . . If in the coming decade we are unable to give it a soul, a spirituality, and a meaning, we will have lost the game." He returned to this topic in a speech made in Strasbourg Cathedral on December 7, 1999, emphasizing the Christian heritage of Europe. "The contribution of Christianity remains essential," he said, "precisely because of the wisdom with which it nourishes its vision of humanity and because of its appeal to the renewal of faith in the values that are the legacy of the Gospel." Romano Prodi, a later president of the European Commission, addressing European churches on October 4, 1999, expressed himself in similar terms: "Europe cannot be conceived without its memories, and in these memories Christianity has left a permanent trace. The different cultures of the European nations, their arts, literature, the hermeneutics of thought have all sprung from the cradle of Christianity, which has nurtured both believers and nonbelievers." And many others have taken the same position.

Why? Because if Europe has a Christian soul, then it has an identity. If Europe has an identity, then a European nation can exist, and if a European nation exists, then a political union can be built. But the crucial decade stressed by Delors has come to an end and Europe is in the same condition as before, if not worse.

So we ask again, why? Why does the process of unification keep running into obstacles? This question has two levels of meaning. The first is superficial and concerns the actual reasons: What are the immediate causes for which the attempts at political unification of Europe have failed or have produced results that in no way approach the desired goal? Usually this question is answered by pointing a finger at the various political intentions of the member states, their divergent interests, the leaders' conflicting ambitions, the people's fears, or the inadequacy of procedures—all the factors that have produced the endless series of paralyses, deaths, and resurrections with which the road to European unification has been paved. This is a technical argument for specialists, and fortunately it is not what we will be concerned with here.[24]

The other level of meaning cuts deeper and refers to *principles*. What are the structural elements underlying the history and current conditions of the whole continent that are an obstacle to its political unification? To answer this question, we must look not to politics but to philosophy, and especially to the liberal doctrine as practiced by the ruling class now engaged with the process of European unification. The answer is precisely what Delors invoked: the lack of a European soul and identity. Principles are stronger than facts. Whereas the facts tell us that European unification failed but might have been successful or might still be successful (if only Europe were more determined, courageous, farsighted, etc.), principles instead say that European unification has failed because it could and cannot but fail. Moreover, the two lines of reasoning—by fact and by principle—differ not only with respect to the cause of the failure but also with respect to possible remedies for it.

If we believe that the causes lie in the contingent motivations of various member states (such as British skepticism, French desire for hegemony, the power of Germany, the fears of the newcomers), then we will seek to remedy the situation solely by taking political action, removing the impediment or striking a compromise. If instead we feel that the cause lies deeper, that it is substantive (and the lack of a European identity is certainly a question of substance), then no political action with the typical tools of politics (a change of leaders, treaties, institutions, voting procedures) will succeed in overcoming the obstacle. In this case, we must reverse the terms. Instead of departing from a constitution in order to create an identity, we should depart from an identity in order to create a constitution. We should not begin with the idea that "Europe is united; now let's give it a soul," but rather with "Let us seek and find the soul of Europe so that unification can happen."

I am convinced of the latter idea. And this brings us back again to the problem of European identity. Does Europe have a single identity? If so, what is that identity?

THE PARADOX OF EUROPEAN IDENTITY

"Identity" is an elusive notion. It is a little like time according to St. Augustine: nobody knows what it is exactly, but everybody knows what you are talking about. Or like certain familiar abstract ideas such as love, friendship, esteem. As long as you don't demand precise definitions for terms like these, everybody knows what you mean.

Certainly the term "identity" has a *moral* connotation. It is like "nation," defined by Ernest Renan as "a soul, a spiritual principle."[25] Sharing an identity with others means sharing with them the same ideal sense of belonging. It means feeling ties of familiarity, solidarity, destiny, obligation, and most especially, love and respect for one's own history, tradition, and land. Identity means identifying oneself but also *distinguishing* oneself: those who say "we" distance themselves necessarily from "the others." When we speak of a European identity, it is to the mingling of such feelings that we must refer. This identity may be complex, highly structured, and stratified, but it must have a single core. If it were merely the sum of many distinct national identities, the result would be, to use Kant's phrase, a "distributive" or "numerical unit," producing an aggregation of peoples, but not *one* people and *one* moral community. Identity is therefore fundamental to the unification of Europe just as the soul is essential to the life of the body.

Conceptually, three strategies have been employed in past attempts to unify Europe.

The first is the spiritual strategy pursued by the founding leaders of Europe when, in the period following the Second World War, the European Community was made up of only six countries. Christianity was their soul of reference. On March 19, 1958, addressing the first European Parliament, Robert Schuman, architect and driving force of the first Community, stated, "All the countries of Europe are permeated by Christian civilization. It is the soul of Europe which must be restored to it."[26] De Gasperi echoed such sentiments when he asked, "How can we conceive of a Europe without Christianity, ignoring its brotherly, social, and humanitarian teachings?"[27] And recalling De Gasperi's efforts in creating a united Europe, Adenauer wrote, "We considered the unification of Europe as the goal of our foreign policy because it was the only way possible to affirm and safeguard our Western, Christian civilization against the fury of totalitarianism."[28]

After this attempt failed, for reasons that we will leave to historians to sort out, the next strategy was an *economic* one. From the soul to the legs, as it were. The underlying argument was: If common institutions (beginning with a common army and a common political assembly) cannot be had, then we should eliminate customs and excise duties, allow peoples to circulate freely in a common market, and wait for economic integration to drag social and political integration along with it. As Jean Monnet said in his address to the first assembly of the European Coal and Steel Community, "Our community is not a coal and steel producers' association: it is the beginning of Europe."[29] But Europeans have never got beyond that beginning. Right in the midst of the most successful period of the economic treaties, the question of giving a soul to Europe was raised once again. So another attempt had to be made, a third strategy implemented. A brief overview of recent events in the process of unification will help us understand this third attempt.

First, the foundation for the *economic* unification of Europe was laid by the treaties of Maastricht (1992) and Amsterdam (1997), which also introduced the idea of European citizenship. Next came *monetary* unification in 1998 with the adoption of the euro. This was followed by *juridical* unification through the ratification of the Charter of Fundamental Rights (Nice, 2000). The last step, which was supposed to bring about the *political* unification of Europe, was the signing of the European Constitution (Rome, 2004), or as the ambiguous title of this document so eloquently reads, the "Treaty Establishing a Constitution for Europe." The Charter of Fundamental Rights, unmodified, became the second part of the Constitution and has been retained in the Treaty of Lisbon (2008), which has since replaced the Constitution, so I will refer to this text as the *European Charter,* or simply as the *Charter,* and I will refer to the authors who drafted the Charter as "the European fathers," or simply "the fathers." (I trust that my readers will not confuse these minor fathers of the European Constitution with the great fathers of the European Community, let alone with the fathers of liberalism discussed in the previous chapter).

Clearly, the fathers were up against a great challenge. The "conventions" that had so ambitiously united them, emulating the American example, had been entrusted with the task of drafting the texts of the Charter of Fundamental Rights and of the European Constitution in the total absence of such vital ingredients as unity of *demos, ethnos,* and the like.[30] Despite the rhetoric used to warm up the atmosphere, the situation here was quite different from what it had been in Philadelphia two centuries earlier. Not only were Madison and Jefferson and all the others absent,[31] but representatives of the people were also missing. The delegates who had come to Brussels were acting in the name of the governments and the national parliaments by which they had been nominated. They were neither representatives elected by the peoples of Europe, nor delegates of the European people or of the European nation (all expressions used with great caution, despite the initial enthusiasm).[32]

Given these circumstances, how could they possibly draw up a European Charter that could capture the European identity (its soul), and breathe life into European patriotism? It was obvious that everything was against such an outcome. In Europe, except in the context of football stadiums when national teams are playing, the very expressions "patriotism" and, worse, "nationalism" still have a sinister ring due to the tragic forms they assumed in the twentieth century. So from the start, this put the writers of the Charter in an uncomfortable situation, because in order to be rid of their old vices, Europeans had to become antinationalistic at home, but to acquire new virtues, they had to be patriotic outside their home turf.

To solve this predicament, the fathers decided to take the only step that seemed reasonable to them: to turn their backs on the past, on the *real history* of the tormented relations among the European states, and look toward the future, with an *ideal design* for a single European nation, or more ambitiously, for a single European state, structured appropriately. Turning one's back on history does not mean forgetting or erasing what has happened, because the real history of Europe—in particular, the recent events of Nazism, fascism, communism, anti-Semitism, and all the rest—can never be forgotten, but it can be overcome, in the sense of the German verb *aufheben*, if we preserve the dark memories and the weight of the past. Turning one's back on history means rather "turning over a new leaf," making a "new start," while remaining well aware that ghosts of the past might still return if the ideal design should fail. It is no wonder that the preamble explicitly but understatedly speaks of "bitter experiences" and "former divisions." Conversely, looking to the future does not mean imagining or dreaming of an abstract plan, but drawing up a precise political project that may unify Europe thanks to its *intrinsic* power of attraction. Therein lies its soul. More precisely, according to the philosophy of the fathers, the soul resides in an appropriate ensemble of principles and values that Europeans cannot help but recognize as fundamental and undeniable. Just as the Constitution stated in listing them all (Article I-2): "The Union is founded on the values of respect for human dignity, freedom, democracy, the rule of law and respect for human rights, including the rights of persons belonging to minorities."

This third strategy of unification is terribly attractive and promising. Once the soul of Europe has been pinned down, formulated clearly, and inserted into the text of the Constitution, the process of political unification ought to have no other obstacles—in principle. Although various leaders may pose resistance (since interests are always lurking around the corner), a trail has been blazed: If Europe has a soul, it has an identity. If it has an identity, then it can be a politically united nation.

The promises were many, but the difficulties in keeping them were equally numerous. Let us limit our discussion to the conceptual difficulties, all of which have the same origin. The "principles" and "indivisible and universal values" stressed in the European Charter transcend by definition any historical-geographical location, and the rights that stem from these principles and values refer to individuals as individuals, that is, independently of their being citizens of one state or another. Therefore, it follows that the Charter, based on universal principles, values, and rights, is a *cosmopolitan* charter and has as its referent the whole human race.

This is a very serious consequence. The fathers were asked to draw up a *European* charter, that is, one for Europeans, and instead they produced a *universal* charter. And it is easy to see why. Inspired by their liberal, democratic spirit and by their fears of nationalism, they jumped from Europeanism to cosmopolitanism.[33] Whether they were aware of it or not,[34] the work they had done, given the inner logic of their approach, created a conceptual paradox that we may call the paradox of European identity, formulated as follows: *Europeans have given themselves a charter, but the European Charter does not identify them as*

Europeans. In other words, Europeans as defined by the Charter are not Europeans as defined by their history.

What had happened and why? What happened was that, since they did not want (and were unable) to build Europe on its history, the fathers decided to build it on an ideal (values and principles). They created a juridical "paradise" appropriately called a "common space," where Europe entered purified, under the form of an abstract community of abstract individuals.[35] It is irrelevant that these individuals have been labeled "European citizens," because it is conceptually extrinsic. "European" is no longer a proper name or a rigid designator; it does not refer to *that* citizen of *that* nation (or "super-nation," or "post-nation") in *that* geopolitical area. Rather, it refers to a member of a vague realm of principles, values, and rights. It is no wonder that many of the discussions concerning European citizenship have hinged on issues regarding the area of application: should it be restricted to native-born Europeans alone, or also conceded to anyone who has lived in Europe for a period of time?[36]

Why this escape into the ideal, where the concrete identity of Europeans vanishes and the notion of European citizenship wears itself so thin it becomes invisible? And once the values and principles have been identified, why not anchor them in some baptismal font of European history? Why not say *these* principles are truly European because they spring from *this* tradition which is truly Europe's own?

Of course, the fathers asked themselves this very question and began searching for that baptismal font. They looked everywhere: in humanism, the Enlightenment, even in socialism, and naturally they thought of Christianity, but they could not agree on this because their liberalism would not let them. As we saw in the previous chapter, today's liberalism is political. It believes that it is possible to found a liberal (and democratic) state without taking into consideration any doctrine of the good. Moreover, as we have seen, this liberalism is secular, and believes that the liberal (and democratic) state need not refer to any religious tradition. Equipped with such a cultural background, the fathers found themselves facing a task in the spirit of Rawls and Habermas: to write a European Charter under a "veil of ignorance" (Rawls) impenetrable to any ethical doctrine, especially a religious doctrine, and to legitimate the nascent European state or super-state "in a self-sufficient way," without any "religious justification" (Habermas). It is easy to see why they chose the doctrine of "constitutional patriotism," which is a facet of political liberalism, for this purpose. But if, as we have tried to show in the previous chapter, liberalism cannot be only political, and if it cannot be secular especially in the widespread sense of "anti-Christian," then the fathers could only fail at their task. Let us try to understand why.

CONSTITUTIONAL PATRIOTISM

No clear, analytical definition has ever been furnished for constitutional patriotism, even though much has been written about it.[37] One author has presented it as the doctrine in which "citizens are thought of as bound to each other by subscription to shared values *rather than by* the more traditional pre-political ties that nation-states have drawn as sources of unity."[38] Habermas, the main theorist but not the inventor of this theory, once described it as follows: "what unites a nation of citizens as opposed to a *Volksnation* is not some primordial substrate but rather an intersubjectively shared context of possible mutual understanding."[39] Let us try to untangle the meaning of these expressions.

Just as political liberalism desires to construct a free state by separating a "general political conception" from a "comprehensive doctrine of the good," constitutional patriotism strives to build a liberal-democratic nation (more precisely, a postmodern nation) by keeping *political* principles and values, such as those that would be inscribed in a political constitution, separate from *pre-political* ethnic, religious, linguistic ties deriving from a people's history. In the case of Europe, constitutional patriotism sets European political citizenship, which is post-national and inclusive, beyond the bounds of ethnic citizenship, which is national and divisive. In other words, its goal is to build a European nation unshackled from the historical or pre-political identity of Europe. Or more simply, to unify Europe by choosing not to address the problem of the soul. An emphatic statement by an Italian scholar cogently expresses the intentions of constitutional patriotism: "No God, Nation, Nature, or History, all terms rigorously spelled with capital letters, are at the origins of the pact, but only the pact itself: voluntary, artificial, and unfounded."[40]

This was obviously manna from heaven for the fathers of the Charter, because such a doctrine promised to help overcome all the typical objections to the unification of Europe: the absence of a *demos,* an *ethnos,* etc., which the Euroskeptics, in politics and in doctrine, have continually raised. As Habermas affirmed, "The prognosis that there cannot be any such thing as a European people remains plausible only if 'the people,' as a source of solidarity, actually depends on some corresponding community as a pre-political basis of trust, which fellow countrymen and women inherit as the shared fate of their socialization."[41] Since constitutional patriotism views the "source of solidarity" of the European people as something that cannot be inherited (because there is no European nation), but must be constructed (through an appropriate charter of shared political principles), the prospects for unification are favorable.

In order to understand where this "source of solidarity" may come from, it is helpful to understand the origins and the initial aim of the doctrine of constitutional patriotism.[42]

This doctrine first arose in Germany on the ruins of Nazi nationalism at a time when the German nation was still divided into two German states. The main problem was: how is it possible to be German and cultivate a sense of German nationalism after Auschwitz? If this were to be done by stressing those traditional elements that historically have inspired feelings of nationhood in Germany and elsewhere—the people, ethnicity, destiny, all that constitutes the *Volksnation*—one would risk repeating the tragedies of recent history. But if those same elements are repudiated, the nation's identity may be endangered.

In the famous *Historikerstreit* of 1986, Habermas harshly criticized any attempt by historians such as Ernst Nolte to explain, contextualize, or historicize Nazism.[43] "If national symbols have lost their influence with the young," Habermas wrote, "if naive identification with one's heritage has yielded to a more tentative relationship to history, if discontinuities are felt more strongly and continuities not celebrated at any price, if national pride and collective self-esteem are filtered through universalist value orientations—to the extent to which all this is really the case, indications of the development of a postconventional identity are increasing."[44]

Moreover, Habermas continued, "the only patriotism that does not alienate us from the West is a constitutional patriotism. Unfortunately, in the cultural nation of the Germans, a connection to universalist constitutional principles that was anchored in convictions could be formed only after—and through—Auschwitz. Anyone who wants to dispel our shame about this fact with an empty phrase like 'obsession with guilt,' anyone who wants to recall the Germans to a conventional form of national identity, is destroying the only reliable basis for our tie to the West."[45] As if to say—and this is an anticipation of the European paradox—that Germans cannot be Germans.

Indeed, the only patriotism that the Germans may be allowed is constitutional patriotism, according to Habermas (rejecting the patriotism of the Deutschmark along with the old nationalism).[46] And in his view, the same holds true for Europeans. It is the only form that they should be allowed if and when they should decide to unite. Not because all Europeans must feel the same sense of "collective responsibility" (NB: "collective responsibility," not "collective guilt") as the Germans feel, but because if Europeans should base their identity on the same kinds of pre-political elements, they would be in danger of forgetting the past and repeating it, just like the Germans.

All feelings of shame aside, the most illustrious precursor of this doctrine was certainly Kant, who was among the earliest supporters of a federation of European states.[47] If we examine it closely, we will see that Habermas's constitutional patriotism promises to fulfill nearly everything proposed by Kant's liberal cosmopolitanism.[48]

First, it promises to make Europeans citizens of a nation on a higher level, a "post-nation" or a "super-nation." If by political decision Europe adopts a single charter, we may assume that the traditional national boundaries will disappear and the states will become one. Next, it promises to extend citizenship to everyone. Anyone (individuals or groups) who shares the principles and values of the European Charter, whatever his or her origin (indigenous or immigrant) and the nature of his or her conception of the public good (metaphysical, rational, moral, religious, etc.), can become a European citizen. (As a corollary, this promises to resolve the problem of integration for the new-comers.) Furthermore, constitutional patriotism promises to fulfill the Kantian dream of a republic built on law and morality (the "kingdom of ends in themselves"). The Charter is a juridical document that contains political principles and ethical values that may be sanctioned through appeal to judicial authority. Finally, constitutional patriotism promises to fulfill Kant's most ambitious dream: "perpetual peace." If everyone enjoys the same right to liberty and the same political rights, and if those rights are respected, then conflicts between European states will cease, just as civil wars within nation-states should cease when they become liberal and democratic.

To sum up: constitutional patriotism promises to give Europe an identity as well as the sense of nationhood it needs in order to unify itself, without drawing on any sources other than strictly political ones. This is exactly how Habermas envisaged it. There is a model for it, which Habermas pointed out and which the European "conventionalists" most certainly had in mind: the United States of America, a union not created on the grounds of a common race, ethnicity, and tradition, but on the patriotism of principles and values shared by the American people. The point is: can this doctrine fulfill all its promises?

No it cannot, at least not in such a formulation, as Habermas soon realized. "The notion of constitutional patriotism appears to many observers to represent too weak a bond to hold together complex societies. The question then becomes even more urgent: under what conditions can a liberal political culture provide a sufficient cushion to prevent a nation of citizens, which can no longer rely on ethnic associations, from dissolving into fragments?"[49]

The reason behind this objection, which is the same objection always raised against every form of cosmopolitanism, is that constitutional patriotism by itself, with its appeal to loyalty toward universal principles and values, is far too weak or *thin* an idea—too generic, abstract, and loosely woven—to create a strong, specific sense of identity, belonging, or loyalty to a single, specific European community.[50] A bridge is needed, a link between the abstract and the concrete, between the ideal and the real, between the supranational and the national, or between the juridical paradise of the Charter and its principles, and the lives of Europeans who must adopt it as their own and give life to it. This link must be something that warms their hearts, stirs their emotions, and produces solidarity; otherwise the Charter will remain something cold and inert, unable to transmute into custom or foster a sense of identity. Without that identity, it cannot arouse in its citizens the feeling of belonging to a nation that is so necessary to Europe's unification.

We must insist on this objection because it is decisive. Until people feel moved to say "I love *my* Europe" or "I am ready to fight to the death to defend *our* Europe," until Europeans have learned to say "We, the people of Europe" or "our country Europe"[51] in the same way that Americans learned to say "We the people of the United States" or "our country," Europe cannot be born. To hasten this birth, a few shared, noble principles written in a document are not enough, especially because it is not clear who has written them on behalf of whom, or for what purpose.[52] Putting it all down in writing is important, but that must come *afterward*.

To overcome this objection, Habermas's idea was to pad the overly cosmopolitan skeleton of constitutional patriotism with European flesh and blood, and thus to consider it not in its *thin* form but in its *thick* one. According to Habermas, *thick* patriotism may be obtained from *thin* patriotism by adding those elements of history and political commitments that are specifically European. Among the former, one such principle is the memory of the Holocaust and of totalitarianism;[53] among the latter, such values as democracy, the welfare state, the environment, and of course peace against what is deemed to be unilateralism and American imperialism.[54] In general, *thin* cosmopolitan patriotism may be transformed into *thick* European patriotism through a process of interpretation and appropriation of those same universal principles by the individual European peoples themselves.

To understand this process better, we may think of it like this: An Italian, French, or German citizen, for example, becomes a fully European citizen, relinquishing a part of his own nationalism, when he comes to cherish the values and principles of Europe defined in the Charter and sees them as the reflection of his own highest tradition, as a shield against the worst parts of his own history, and as a means of fulfilling his own noblest aspirations. When that happens, the European Charter will become a mirror in which he will see a double image of himself: first as a European who shares the same principles with all other Europeans, and second as a member of his own nation—Italian, French, German, etc.—whose history and ideals are absorbed, entirely or in part, by those principles. Or we may think of the Charter as Newton's prism refracting a ray of light. The white light of Europe breaks down into a rainbow (the national identities) as it strikes the different planes of the prism (the histories and traditions). As Habermas writes, "The political culture of a country crystallizes around its constitution. Each national culture develops a distinctive interpretation of those constitutional principles that are equally embodied in other republican constitutions—such as popular sovereignty and human rights—in light of its own national history. A 'constitutional patriotism' based on these interpretations can take the place originally occupied by nationalism."[55]

Truly manna from heaven for every believer in Europe, because this doctrine gives him a double gift: a European nation separate and distinct from any pre-political European identity, and a European patriotism different from the nationalisms of the European countries. As Habermas commented, "it is to be expected that the political institutions that would be created by a European constitution would have a catalytic effect."[56] Or as another scholar has remarked, "The EU . . . might fit a notion of a constitution as an ongoing project actually much more closely than constitutions at the level of the nation-state."[57]

If that is true, then European unification can be achieved. An enlightened convention of few members first approves the principles; the rest will be done by the people themselves, over time. All that is needed are political determination, adherence to the liberal and democratic principles outlined in the Charter, educational initiatives to make those principles understood by the people, and enough time for the "source of solidarity" to have a "catalytic effect."

Unfortunately this won't happen. Constitutional patriotism is not "self-sufficient" or thick enough to construct a nation or European state. Something is missing. If we examine the doctrine critically, we will see what that is.

THE ETHICAL DEFICIT: THE HUMAN PERSON

The separation of patriotism and nationalism is certainly attractive. Who would not want to enjoy all the positive attributes usually ascribed to the former without having to deal with the negative aspects of the latter? And what a bargain. Who wouldn't like to "give Europe a soul," for the cheap price of simply accepting a charter of common principles and values? And more generally, who wouldn't like to see the entire West united? Everybody would. But can we have a patriotism *without* the elements characteristic of nationalism? This is the same question we asked in the first chapter: can liberalism stand without a doctrine of the good or a religion? The answer is no. The process of European unification within the terms of constitutional patriotism confirms this fact. We cannot avoid addressing the problem of the soul, of finding a pre-political baptismal font specific to Europe and originating therein. A debate held in January 2004 between Habermas and Joseph Ratzinger, now Pope Benedict XVI, will help us understand why.

Opening the debate, Habermas acknowledged that from the viewpoint of *national* patriotism "the claim of positive law to validity would need to be based on those pre-political ethical convictions of religions or national communities."[58] Consistent with his position, he reiterated that this cannot be valid for a *supranational* (or post-traditional) constitutional state, which is what Europe needs. Such a supranational state, precisely because it lacks its own *demos, ethos,* etc., is "committed to neutrality in terms of its world view."[59] Therefore, it cannot take for its foundation any specific pre-political, ethical, or religious conception. What such a state needs, Habermas continues, is an "*autonomous* justification and that all the citizens can *rationally* accept the claim this justification makes."[60]

What does this mean? According to Habermas, "Political liberalism . . . understands itself as a nonreligious and postmetaphysical justification of the normative bases of the democratic constitutional state. This theory is in the tradition of a rational law that renounces the 'strong' cosmological or salvation-historical assumptions of the classical and religious theories of the natural law."[61] There is no need to seek a foundation in "pre-political ethical convictions of religious or national communities."[62] There is no need for any "natural law,"[63] because if democratic procedures are seen "as a method whereby legitimacy is generated by legality, there is no 'deficit of validity' that would need to be filled by the ethical dimension,"[64] and also because "the democratic procedure for the production of law evidently forms the *only* postmetaphysical source of legitimacy."[65] As we were saying in the previous chapter, political liberalism subscribes to the secular equation: it has no ethical basis, and in particular no religious basis.

But this is not true. In constitutional patriotism, as in political liberalism, the deficit of validity that Habermas denies does indeed exist. Argumentation and democratic procedures are not enough to fill this deficit precisely because it is a deficit of an "ethical dimension," and that is an ethical deficit. The essential point is that "If the process of democratic legislation demands that the basic liberal and political rights be granted simultaneously,"[66] then, to what Habermas describes as "'weak' suppositions about the normative contents of the communicative constitution of socio-cultural forms of life,"[67] and to what he calls "the pragmatic presuppositions of argumentation,"[68] we must add the *strong* supposition, which is axiological and not procedural, that communicative practice takes place among *persons* who recognize each other as such.

To simplify: if argumentation among citizens is the tool for the founding and sharing of their political constitution (the "method whereby legitimacy is generated by legality") since this constitution is liberal and democratic and thus contains values regarding them first and foremost as individuals (for example: equality, tolerance, respect), then argumentation requires that each individual recognize the others, tolerate and respect them, feel equal to them, attribute dignity to them, and so on. This means that each individual must treat every other individual as a *person,* or in Kantian terms, as *an end in itself.* Since this is clearly a *moral* obligation, it must be added to the logical, pragmatic, and procedural obligations of argumentation by which it cannot be substituted.

Habermas claims that "to the extent that the democratic process satisfies the conditions for an inclusive and discursive formation of opinion and will, it establishes an assumption that the results will be rationally acceptable."[69] That is true, but only if those who wish to communicate with others also recognize them as moral peers. The rational and procedural foundation of the liberal democratic state as viewed by Habermas (and by the fathers of the European Charter) does not proceed from this prior recognition of others as persons, and does not mention any additional moral suppositions. This is the ethical deficit. It is the same ethical deficit we find in political liberalism when it considers itself to be "self-sufficient." Those who participate in Rawls' hypothetical "original situation" must regard themselves and be regarded by others not as simple, naked, rational individuals, but as moral subjects. The "veil of ignorance" cannot hide interlocutors' essential quality as moral persons.

Here we draw closer to the crux of constitutional patriotism, political liberalism, and secular Europe. Where does our concept of the person originate? It does not derive from the practice of argumentation, because it is a presupposition for that practice.[70] It does not derive from democratic procedures allowed by institutions, because these take the idea of the person as their point of reference. Clearly it derives from *outside* the practice of argumentation or democratic procedures. The concept of the person, or the end in itself, i.e. that each individual must be respected because as an individual he is endowed with dignity, is a *pre*-political and obviously *non*-political concept. It is a concept of an *ethical-religious* nature, and more precisely, it is a *Christian* concept. It follows that, just as liberalism cannot be self-sufficient, constitutional patriotism cannot separate itself from pre-political elements. If constitutional patriotism is to support the European Charter, it cannot set aside the pre-political elements of European history, and particularly its ethical Christian and religious elements.

Cardinal Ratzinger replied to Habermas, "[In Europe] there are no longer any motivations for our great ethical principles or for human dignity, and we have finally ended up with positivism because Habermas' constitutional patriotism is positivism. The constitution by itself produces morality. But that is untrue. It cannot do so, it needs powers from the past and we must find and reawaken those powers."[71] This is true. Constitutional patriotism is constitutional positivism. Presenting its principles as procedural and discursive axioms cannot change its substance. In the view of Habermas, it is the Charter that produces identity, and not the other way around.

Thus the ethical deficit of constitutional patriotism (and of the Charter, which has adopted its philosophy) must be filled. But with what shall it be filled? There is no doubt that in speaking of the "powers from the past" Cardinal Ratzinger was referring to the Judeo-Christian tradition. It is in this tradition that the concept of the person, endowed with dignity because it was created in the image of God, sinks its deepest roots. If constitutional patriotism wishes to become *thick* and relevant to Europe, and appropriate for its history, why not fill its deficit with an appeal to that tradition? Why not recognize Christianity as its own basis or as a part of itself? The official answer is that any reference to its history would be divisive and not inclusive. But the real answer is: because liberal European culture accepts the secular equation and rejects Christianity.[72] But by doing so, and in the absence of adequate substitutes (constitutional patriotism is not an adequate substitute because it contains a deficit it cannot fill), liberal European culture can produce no notion of European identity, either religious or secular. In the end, it opposes the very thing it wishes to promote: the unification of Europe.

THE POVERTY OF SECULARISM

Actually, Habermas was not unaware of the importance of Christianity in the forming of Europe and in the constructing of the liberal state. In an essay interview published a few years before his debate with Cardinal Ratzinger, he wrote:

> *Christianity has functioned for the normative self-understanding of modernity as more than a mere precursor or catalyst. Egalitarian universalism, from which sprang the ideas of freedom and social solidarity, of an autonomous conduct of life and emancipation, of the individual morality of conscience, human rights and democracy, is the direct heir to the Judaic ethic of justice and the Christian ethic of love. This legacy, substantially unchanged, has been the object of continual critical appropriation and reinterpretation. To this day, there is no alternative to it. And in light of the current challenges of a postnational constellation we continue to draw on the substance of this heritage. Everything else is just idle postmodern talk.[73]*

Here Habermas recognized explicitly that for the unification of Europe, Christianity was not merely a "precursor" or a "catalyst," but also a fountainhead that continues to nurture us. But he wavered (disconcerting his secularist followers, and never satisfying his religious or secular critics). There was a profound reason for this. The admission that Christianity functions as the source of liberal democracy is at odds with the main tenet of Habermas's philosophical system, according to which the foundation of the constitutional liberal democratic state can and must be "autonomous" or "self-sufficient," because it can and must be exclusively "procedural" or "rational," or "argumentative." Admitting that Christianity is a valid basis for European unification contradicts constitutional patriotism, which intends to erase any and all pre-political elements, especially religious ones, from unification.

Like Croce before him in "Why We Cannot Help Calling Ourselves Christians," Habermas found himself standing at the crossroads, unable to make up his mind. Like Croce, he recognized that without Christianity neither Europe nor Western civilization could have existed. Like Croce, he came close to admitting that Christianity is not only the historical fountainhead of this civilization, but also its conceptual and theoretical foundation. Like Croce, who claimed that "in our own times our thought inevitably works on the lines laid down by Christianity," he admits, as we have just seen, that "to this day, there is no alternative to it." But Habermas, like Croce, is unable to decide. On one hand, his system compels him to remove Christianity from the foundations of liberalism, because it is a substantive element that cannot be reduced to argumentative or procedural factors. His system also compels him to remove mention of it from the European Charter, because it is a pre-political element. On the other hand, the moral sensibility he has recently displayed[74] seems to compel him to regard Christianity as the basis of liberalism and to treat it as the baptismal act of Europe. As we have seen, Croce could never completely decide between the two, and thus he flung his philosophical system wide open to an irresolvable contradiction. Habermas finds himself in this same position. His discursive foundation of the liberal democratic state is secular, but his way of filling the ethical deficit of that foundation is Christian. His theory that "the liberal state has an interest in the free expression of religious voices in the public arena and in the political participation of religious organizations"[75] is correct, but incompatible with the idea that a liberal state may found itself with the tool of argumentation. If the liberal state could truly be self-founding, why should it be "interested" in other voices or sources?

The European Charter does not neglect the concept of the person. The preamble refers to "the inviolable and inalienable rights of the human person." Article I-2 of the Constitution proclaims that "the Union is founded on the values of respect for human dignity." The Charter does, however, turn a blind eye to the Christian history of this concept and the function it has played in European society. Is it possible the fathers did not know this? That they had forgotten Dante and his dream of a Christian empire—or Erasmus and his Christian cosmopolitanism, or Locke and his Christian natural rights, or Kant and his ethical Christian state, or Benedetto Croce and his secular Christianity? Is it possible that they had never visited a Christian place of worship or had never noticed how the urban layouts of European cities and towns are always structured around a chapel, a church, a basilica? Could they fail to notice that a cross always stands in the center of our towns, villages, and cities?

No. Yet the fathers were learned men: politicians, jurists, historians, constitutionalists of the finest caliber. They were well versed in Greek culture, Roman law, the history of Europe and of the West. Of course they were well aware that there was no solution to the paradox of European identity unless a source, a great taproot, a specific tradition were found to which the Charter could be anchored. If they failed to address this issue, it was not from ignorance, but intentional.[76] This intellectually depressing story has been told so often that we need only trace the main plot here. The fathers had to perform a balancing act on the tightrope of hypocritical language. They lacked the courage to call things by their real names.

Let us look at the wording of the texts. The Charter of Fundamental Rights (2000) says that the Union is "conscious of its spiritual and moral heritage," without saying just what heritage it means. The preamble to the Constitution (2004) goes a step further in saying that the Union has drawn "inspiration from the cultural, religious, and humanist inheritance of Europe," but does not specify exactly what this inheritance is. The same formula appears in the Treaty of Lisbon (2008), which took the place of the rejected Constitution. In all these cases, reading between the somewhat crooked lines, we see an obvious intent to erase the Christian history of Europe. The apostasy of Christianity embraced by the European mainstream and the "postmodern talk" that Habermas stressed are pushing in this direction.

The culture of Europe today is not exactly secular. It is strongly ideological, averse to criticism, intolerant of objections, resistant to contradiction, impervious to contrary arguments. It is an antireligious culture. It treats religion as superstition, as a vestige of a mythological era, as the legacy of a remote time in human history, as the leavings of intellectual immaturity. After the decline of ideologies, European secularism has continued to drink at the founts of Marx, Nietzsche, Freud, and other proponents of "atheist humanism," as described by Henri de Lubac.[77] Secularism makes continual appeal to Galileo, but does not appreciate the distinction between the truth of science and the truth of faith, which Galileo himself appropriately introduced, and instead tries to carry the latter into the tribunal of the former.[78] The only contribution of Christianity that secularism is willing to admit is the consolation of the foolish—a bit like magic, astrology, fairy tales, or quaint stories for the gullible.

In my next chapter, I will be discussing the causes and consequences of the antireligious culture that is overwhelming the liberal state. Here I will just point out the threat it poses not only to European unification, but also to the survival of Western civilization as a whole.

First, it is not true that secularism makes Europeans cosmopolitan; rather, it makes them stateless. Who are we? If we cannot even define ourselves as children of the "Christian continent" and as heirs to the Judeo-Christian tradition, which more than any other force has shaped our history, then we can reply to this question at best by pointing to a spot on the map. And that too is difficult, because where there are no clear connotations, there are no definite denotations. The debate over Turkey's entry into the European Union shows us how things stand. By concealing our history in the name of secularism, we have allowed secularism to disguise our own identity from us. Secularism offers us only a negative identity: it tells us what we are *not*, what we *don't* want to be, but doesn't say anything about *who we are* or *what we believe in.*

Moreover, it is untrue that by disguising or denying our identity, secularism will improve our relationships with others. Leaving aside the question of multiculturalism and Islam, which I will discuss at length in the next chapter, we should note that secularism separates Europe from the rest of the West, especially from America. Today Europe is drifting away from America because it does not understand or appreciate America, most particularly the American conviction of being a people chosen by God with ideals to realize and a religious mission to fulfill: *One nation under God.*[79] Between Europe and America, the translator's manual is long out of date; the same words can have two very different meanings depending on which side of the Atlantic you are on.

To name a few illustrative cases: What is called "civil religion" in America is called "sanctimoniousness," if not "fundamental-ism," in Europe. What is called "expansion of civilization" or "promotion of democracy" in America is called "imposition of a lifestyle," the American way of life, in Europe. What is called "exportation of democracy" in America is translated as "impe-rialist aggression" in Europe. What is called "universalism of rights" in America is called "masked ethnocentrism" in Europe. And so on for every relevant expression or term. It is no wonder, then, that what is called "right to self-defense" in America is called "recourse to the UN" in Europe.[80]

This is where the apostasy of Christianity is leading Europe, far from its own tradition and religion, far from the West, and in the end, far from its identity and from itself.

WHY EUROPE SHOULD CALL ITSELF CHRISTIAN

It has rightly been pointed out that the idea of Europe precedes the idea of European identity, and that the European identity has changed throughout the centuries.[81] This is true. But it has never changed with respect to one point: the dialectic of "us/them." Like all other identities, the European identity has been structured and continues to be structured upon this concept. The actors may have changed, but the logic has not. In Europe, "them" referred to the "pagans" during the barbarian invasions; then to the "infidels" at the time of the wars with Islam; then to the "savages" in the age of geographical discovery; and now to the "fundamentalists" of our own time. Yet for centuries, since the time that the Roman Empire was being Christianized, in every dealing with "them"—in peace or war, through missions or conquests, accommodating or submissive—that "us" has always and invariably referred to a Christian matrix: in Rome when the empire fell and the popes stopped the barbarians; at Poitiers (732), Granada (1492), Lepanto (1571), and Vienna (1683), when Europe defended itself against Islam; and wherever Christianity was transported, in North and South America, China, India, Africa. This was the baptismal font of European civilization: *In the beginning was the Gospel.*[82]

True, before "the beginning" there were other things as well. There was ancient Rome, and before that there was Athens. But Athens and Rome did not cancel out Bethlehem, nor does Bethlehem cancel out Jerusalem. Christianity is the soul of Europe not because it has refrained from mixing with other cultures, but because it led them to unity, structured and shaped them, welded them together into a single terrain, the land where Peter and Paul disembarked—the "Christian continent." This process of absorption, integration, and fusion is so keenly felt by Christians that Pope Benedict XVI was moved to speak of the "profound harmony between what is Greek in the best sense of the word and the biblical understanding of faith in God," and of a "synthesis between the Greek spirit and the Christian spirit," and even of "the Greek heritage [as] an integral part of Christian faith."[83] Christianity collects the waters of many rivers in one great ocean.

The tradition of Europe is decidedly a composite one. Without the reasoning of the Greeks, we would not have had those forms of thought that are the pillars of our methods of argumentation, beginning with modern science. Without Roman law, we would not have those associated life forms that inspire our public institutions, including our democracy. Yet without the laws of Moses and the sacrifice of Christ, our arguments would not be respectful and our institutions would not be liberal and democratic. As Tocqueville affirmed, "the advent of Jesus Christ upon earth was required to teach that all members of the human race are by nature equal and the like."[84]

Yes, Europeans descend from three hills—Mt. Sinai, the Acropolis, Golgotha; and they have three capitals—Athens, Rome, Jerusalem. But Christianity has baptized them. If Europe is without a soul today, it has not always been so. Not that it was ever deprived of one; rather, it has refused the one that history has given it.

Nor are there other formulas that might better define the European identity or produce better results.

It has been said that Europe is "united in diversity," which is the motto of the European Union. Or that Europe is a "mongrelism of cultures."[85] Or that it is "a union without 'us.'"[86] All these formulas focus on one point or another while remaining vague. Do they mean to say *what Europe is* or *what Europe ought to be?* Perhaps both, but even though the description may be correct, the recommendation associated with it is not in the interests of Europe or to the benefit of its political unification.

Europe has also been described as "a continent of energetic mongrels."[87] From a racial point of view this is true, but from a cultural standpoint a "mongrel" identity is no identity at all. The same holds true for the formula "a union without 'us.'" Without "us" there can be no "them," or perhaps there can be no one but "them." Without a European identity, there would be no boundaries, no distinctions between European citizens, refugees, immigrants, guests, tourists, and passersby. Those who favor the political unification of Europe say that they don't want it to be "against" anyone. They want it to be open, inclusive, tolerant, respectful, peaceful, but they cannot seriously imagine that a united Europe can come into being without distinctions and demarcations. The very logic of integration presupposes that along with the subject to be integrated we also have a subject that does the integrating. Integrating is not the same thing as hosting or aggregating. To integrate is to assume that we have something—an identity—that means enough to us that we want others to respect and appreciate it, and to share it with us.

Naturally, notions such as "mongrelism of cultures" or "a union without 'us'" are not accidental, but refer to serious problems faced by Europe today. Such expressions may originate from good intentions, but sometimes also from fears. Those good intentions are related to the act of welcoming and integrating others; and the fears, to the concern that Europeans may have to bear the consequences. A large part of European culture is so paralyzed by the idea of a civilizational clash with Islam, and by the memory of the religious wars, that they would do *anything*, even deny that Europe is a civilization with its own religion, in order to avoid conflicts and to keep from appearing "aggressive" or closed to "dialogue." Unfortunately, this does not lead to European identity or to the unification of Europe, but rather to the surrender of Europe and the loss of what it means to be European.

There are those who believe that "secular Europe will have real advantages in an increasingly fundamentalist world. It can become a continent where reason and science—drawing on the principles of Europe's earlier Enlightenment—can flourish, enhancing medicine, the environment, and human rights. . . . Europe's secular approach . . . will help superpower Europe to avoid the kind of universalist, moralizing Christianity which fuelled old British colonialism and modern Republican American foreign policy."[88]

Others wonder, "does it make any difference in daily life whether Europeans still believe in God or go to church?"[89] And there are those who believe that the question of identity isn't all that important: "Although some federalists still dream of a country called Europe, and the European Union sometimes pretends to be a state with its own flag, passport and anthem, it is fundamentally different from a state. Like Visa, it is a decentralized network that exists to serve its member-states."[90]

Europe, these people are all saying, is sui generis, unique. And it's true. The definitions of Europe given by scholars are usually approximations (an "open continent") or aspirations (an "oasis of peace") or negations (the "not-America")[91] or double negations ("Neither Reich nor Nation").[92] The positive definitions are all indefinite, analogical or allusive, referring to the complex nature of European institutions (the "Visa network," for example) or to the Union's system of government ("neo-medieval empire").[93] Although these formulas hit on more than one good point, they transform the problem into its solution. If, to answer the question "Europe is . . . ," the *definiens* turns out to be a rephrasing of the *definiendum,* then it has no explanatory or predictive power, but simply attests to the current state of things.

At the end of the first chapter, I laid down ten reasons why liberals should call themselves Christians. Half of those reasons are valid for Europe as well. Europe *should* call itself Christian—

1) If it desires unification. In order to be united, Europe must have *a* people, *an* identity, and it must feel that it is *one* nation. Europe today doesn't feel anything like this, and the attempt to fill the missing sense of nationhood with the surrogate of a patriotism of principles to which people should feel emotionally attached is producing no results, because no one

feels attachments in the abstract. A soul is necessary in order to stir emotion. What is needed is a Christian soul.

2) If it wishes to affirm itself as the civilization of basic human rights. From the Declaration of the Rights of Man and the Citizen (1789) to the European Convention for the Protection of Human Rights and Freedoms (1950) and to the European Charter of Fundamental Rights (2000), Europe has "recognized"—this is the word that is always used—that people have fundamental rights and freedoms as human beings, rather than as members of states. This recognition is the secular homage that Europe pays to the Christian tradition.

3) If it truly desires to defend itself and avoid religious wars or clashes of civilization. Today, Europe is under violent attack by Islamic fundamentalism and under pressure from Islamic immigration. Its typical reaction has been to recite a mea culpa, adding a "but clause" at the end. Did terrorists carry out massacres in Madrid and London, and in places where Europeans go on vacation? Abominable, *but* American imperialism is also a form of terrorism. Do they rob and murder? Certainly reprehensible acts, *but* don't forget they are fighting for the liberation of their countries; they treat hostages kindly; they don't harm women. Do they use kamikazes? Indeed, a crime against humanity, *but* they do it out of desperation. Are they still killing Christians? That's awful, *but* they must protect themselves from being proselytized. Are they attacking our embassies and demonstrating in our cities? How very uncivil of them, *but* they were provoked by a satirical cartoon, or a film or a book or a political speech or a lecture by the pope. And so on. By reaffirming its Christian identity, Europe will not be making a gesture of arrogance or hostility toward others. On the contrary, this is the very condition under which dialogue with others can take place and true integration can occur.

4) If it wishes to put the tragic season of the recent past behind it. No degree of material well-being, scientific progress, or technological development could ever protect Europeans from the dangers of the Holocaust, concentration camps, or gulags. Europe had never seen as much progress as it did in the days when these hideous events occurred. Paganism is not a source of democracy, despite what some European politicians may have said. Freedom cannot be nourished by agnosticism, atheism, secularism. If we desire peace, coexistence, and respect, we must believe in the values on which these depend. The values of Christianity are still the best antidote to prevarications of all kinds, including those perpetrated in the name of these same values.

5) If it intends to overcome its present moral crisis. After so much antireligious enlightenment and anti-Christian secularism, Europe today feels insecure, uncertain, worried. Perhaps Europeans are not rushing back to their churches in droves, but they are rediscovering them. They are beginning to feel the moral uneasiness and the spiritual vacuum that recent popes, not political leaders, have repeatedly denounced.

Europeans are beginning to realize that the apostasy of Christianity acts like a drug. First it induces the euphoria of omnipotence, but then it provokes exhaustion and frustration. If Europe repudiates Christianity, any attempt at unification is doomed to fail, for it will have no solid or lasting core to hold it together.

Quod erat demonstrandum.

CHAPTER THREE

Relativism, Fundamentalism, and the Question of Morals

"BETTER": ARE WE ALLOWED TO USE THAT WORD?

In the first chapter, we addressed the theoretical and political crisis of liberalism and concluded that it could be solved by attributing an ethical and specifically Christian basis to liberal doctrine. In the second chapter, we discussed the current stalemate in the process of European unification and the risks to social cohesion now endangering the West, concluding that in order to solve that crisis, Europe and the West need to recover their traditional Christian identity. Here one may ask: Well, why not abandon liberalism to its crisis and replace it with another political doctrine or regime? Why not leave Europe as it is—or why not try to unify it in some other way? Couldn't we live without liberalism, a united Europe, and a cohesive West?

My answer to the second question is: of course we could. Perhaps Europe's future wouldn't be a rosy one, but it could keep on just as it is. Many people think so and are only trying to get by as best they can, some with conviction, others merely resigned.

The question regarding liberalism cuts deeper. The liberal doctrine continues to shape Western states, economies, and societies. The main ideas of liberalism—basic rights, the separation of powers, a distinction between the state and civil society, the separation of church and state, the market economy—have established themselves in many countries and provide the basis for Western lifestyles. Granted, there is no conclusive argument proving that liberal regimes are "the end of history" or a necessary goal. Nor has it been proved that globalization is equivalent to Westernization. It is a fact, however, that liberal regimes are continually expanding, that they attract many people, and that they keep making great progress in terms of guarantees, opportunities, growth, and well-being. Thus when asked "Could we live without liberalism?" we are puzzled, because it is almost like being asked if we could live without the free market, science, technology, or democracy. It is hard to imagine what other system could replace liberal regimes to our equal satisfaction, because the conviction is ingrained in us that they are better than any other regime in existence or even imaginable.

Did I say *better?*

Here we jump from a problem into a trap. The problem is that judgments such as "X is better than Y" are difficult to make with reference to lifestyles, cultures, traditions, or civilizations. The trap is the notion that we shouldn't even try to make them. The trap is decidedly odd because it applies selectively according to the situation. For example: No one complains if we say that the European way of life is better than the American one, or vice versa. Millions of men and women on both sides of the Atlantic are busy formulating such judgments day in and day out. A vast specialized literature exists on the subject, churned out continually by economists, jurists, sociologists, and other academics.

However, no one is allowed to say that the European or American way of life is better than the Indian, or the Chinese, or especially the Islamic way of life. Everyone thinks so, but no one dares say so. If they do, they are criticized, or rather, heckled, rebuked, even punished as if they had expressed an offensive, unseemly, or illicit opinion. A ferocious watchdog called "politically correct language" is unleashed upon them, reducing them to silence. This sort of Minotaur acts as an ethical custodian, a praetorian guard to protect the official line.

Although this politically correct language appears to be courteous, it is often hypocritical and conceals a subtle violence. First, it forces us not to call things by their real names in terms of sex, gender, disabilities, skin color, culture, or religious customs. Next, it disguises problems, or points us toward wrong solutions, or toward solutions that people don't want. If, for example, we are not allowed to say that in a certain ethnic community there is a high crime rate and high dropout rate, or that a certain sexual behavior transmits disease, then you may not take suitable measures of correction or protection, or perhaps the ones you do take may turn out to be counterproductive, acting only upon the effects and not upon the causes. If you call an act of terrorism a "man-caused disaster," you probably don't understand the true nature of the phenomenon and won't use adequate means to put a stop to it. Or, to give another example, if you call a child's father "Parent A" and its mother "Parent B," then you suggest that the more familiar forms of paternity or maternity can be replaced by others deviating from those that occur in nature. Lastly, politically correct language goes against our deepest intuitions. Not only does it blur distinctions, dulcify and correct expressions that may at times need rethinking, but it also limits our use of some handy words that we employ every day in common speech.[1] "Better" is one of them.

A liberal English scholar has written:

Virtually everybody in Britain believes, and rightly, that whatever the shallowness and injustices of European life, it is superior to that of most other cultures. This powerful conviction results not merely from the fact that it happens to be the way of life with which we are familiar. It also arises because we regard our apparatus of rights and the rule of law as better than the Islamic Shariah for example. Nor do we regard our disapproval of the ritual genital mutilation of young girls, something prevalent in parts of East Africa, as a mere local prejudice. Nor do we think our notions of equality of opportunity have much to learn from the caste societies of the Indian sub-continent. Nor are we commonly going in search of many lessons about the decent treatment of women, and of political prisoners, from the Chinese. Indeed, we hardly need to pose these questions theoretically before practice tells us the answer: millions of outsiders are beating on our doors trying to get in, and there is no reverse traffic.[2]

Personally, I agree, and for the very same reasons. I will also add that the European and Western situation is better than any other, particularly but not only that of the Islamic world, with respect to law, institutions, constitutions, and political regimes. A free parliament is better than a great *ummah*; a political and electoral struggle better than a *jihad*. Citizenship is better than *dhimmitude*. A democracy is better than the *shariah*; a court sentence better than a *fatwah,* etc. So as to our conviction that "we" are better than "they" are, a belief widely held and defended—why are we not allowed to affirm it publicly?

Perhaps out of courtesy: it is impolite to call attention to others' shortcomings; a pinch of insincerity often makes for a smoother coexistence. Or perhaps out of hospitality: if the others are guests in our home, we should keep from raising embarrassing questions concerning our differences. Perhaps out of the desire to seek our own advantage: we need others for our own well-being, therefore we try to avoid treading on their toes. Or maybe out of fear: because others are strong and threatening, we feel it wise not to judge them or interfere, in order to avoid conflict. And so on.

These reasons are all easily understandable and respectable; all human coexistence requires a minimum of mutual adaption. But they are also superficial reasons, concealing a deeper one, which has less to do with good manners or the desire to seek our own advantage, than with the political application of a dominant doctrine.

This doctrine says: not only is the relationship "better than" difficult to evaluate when applied to social ways of living, it is impossible to establish, except in the case of lifestyles descending from common roots or belonging to a much wider, shared way of life, as in the case of Europe and America. And if this relationship cannot be established, any attempt to evaluate it is arbitrary—and therefore arrogant, presumptuous, unseemly, reproachable.

The application of this doctrine asserts: if within a society there are groups with different lifestyles, cultures, traditions, and religions, and these lifestyles cannot be ranked as "better" or "worse" on a common scale, then the groups must be left free to choose for themselves how they want to live (as long as no harm is done to others), and the greater society must embrace them all.

This doctrine is called *relativism*. Its application is called *multiculturalism*. Widely praised and practiced, these are two temptations with which liberalism is flirting today. Both are implicated in the moral crisis of Europe and the West, and both are indefensible in theory and harmful in practice.

This is what I will be dealing with in this chapter. First I will examine the doctrine of relativism and the practice of multiculturalism. Next I will try to show that they pose an obstacle to solving one of the most difficult challenges Europe is now facing: the integration of immigrants. Then I will discuss the other dramatic problem threatening the West today: Islam and Islamic fundamentalism. I will attempt to show that relativism and multiculturalism not only are unable to solve this threat, but actually make it worse. I will maintain that dialogue with Islam, though difficult, is indeed possible, but *not* in the form of interreligious dialogue. Lastly, I will look at what the combining of relativism with democracy has done to the old liberal state and will examine the risks of further degeneration threatening liberal states, especially in the field of ethics. I will find yet another reason why we should call ourselves Christians.

RELATIVISM

The core of relativism says: "There is no single true morality. There are many different moral frameworks, none of which is more correct than the others."[3] This view has several corollaries.

For example, (a) moral truth does not exist; (b) there is no common scale of values by which we may commensurate diverse values; (c) transcultural values do not exist; (d) no solution to value conflicts is valid everywhere. Last, the toughest and most paradoxical theory: if none of the above exists, then (e) no value system, when judged from within its own confines—which is the only perspective from which it may be judged—can be pronounced better or worse than any other.

All this derives from the undeniable fact of the *plurality* of values, and from the inescapable problem of *comparing* them. As there are many value systems, and as different cultures have different value systems and different hierarchies for the same values, is there a common measure with which they may be evaluated altogether?

The plurality of values was not unknown to the fathers of liberalism. As we saw in the first chapter, their main problem, and the main problem of all liberals, was how to ensure attachment and loyalty to the state on the part of individuals, who, being free and equal, have different conceptions of the good. The fathers were optimistic and thought that pluralism, even religious pluralism, was not earth-shattering. "But it does me no injury," wrote Thomas Jefferson, "for my neighbor to say there are twenty gods or no God. It neither picks my pocket nor breaks my leg."[4] He asked, "Is uniformity of opinion desirable? . . . Is uniformity attainable?" No, it isn't, and compulsion would not help attain it in any case. "Reason and free enquiry are the only effectual agents against error. Give a loose to them and they will support the true religion by bringing every false one to their tribunal, to the test of their investigation."[5] Jefferson went on to affirm that "if a sect arises whose tenets would subvert morals, good sense has fair play and reasons and laughs it out of doors, without suffering the state to be troubled with it."[6]

Nor did the fathers think the problem was unsolvable. As we have seen, Locke thought that "the state of nature has a law of nature to govern it, which obliges everyone: and reason, which is that law, teaches all mankind, who will but consult it, that being all equal and independent, no one ought to harm another in his life, health, liberty, or possessions."[7] Conceptions of the good are many, but all can and must be compared with the natural rights that have been "planted" in the minds of men.[8] In the Declaration of Independence, Jefferson referred to "self-evident" truths and maintained that a government is legitimate only when "laying its foundations on such principles." Similarly, Kant claimed that there are principles common to all humanity: the principles of morality, of the republican constitution, and of the ethical state serve as criteria to evaluate personal maxims and political institutions. For example, "the idea of a constitution in harmony with the natural right of human beings, one namely in which the citizens obedient to the law, besides being united, ought also to be legislative, lies at the basis of all political forms."[9]

The Romantic and idealist reaction to the views of Kant and others radically changed the solution to the problem. Their new approach anticipated today's relativism: there is *no* one single principle—metaphysical, ethical, or rational—that can bind together the whole of humanity. There are only historical cultures, each with its own principles, values, and hierarchies.

To cite a few examples: Hegel's critique of Kant's categorical imperative was an effort to historicize or contextualize values and rights (today we would say, to render them "communal" rather than universal).[10] Other criticisms were oriented toward relativism. Kant had spoken of the "critique of reason," but Hamann objected that "the first purification of reason consisted in the partly misunderstood, partly failed attempt to make reason independent of all tradition and custom and belief in them."[11] Kant had asserted that reason is "universal," but Hamann replied that reason is clothed in or even constituted by language, which is "the only, first, and last *organon* and criterion of reason with no credentials but tradition and usage."[12] Kant had claimed that reason is "legislator," and Jacobi pointed out that reason, while legislating, is moved by interests and thus by circumstances and culture. Kant had imagined a civil constitution of universal value, while Herder objected that this was ethnocentrism because it meant projecting our standards upon others: "It is terrible arrogance to affirm that to be happy, everyone must become European."[13]

With regard to these positions, what's new in relativism today is only a question of tone, or particularly of measure. In order to contextualize values and rights, the idealistic and Romantic relativist sought refuge in the idea of the nation, the people, local culture, communities that shape individuals, create their rights and establish the bounds within which they may be exercised. The contemporary relativist, who has passed through Nietzsche and the tragedies of the dictatorships, rejects even these ways out. His conclusion tends toward subjectivism, skepticism, nihilism, and the deconstruction of any concept claiming to be universal, or any institution aspiring to be transcultural. Thus, as Nietzsche said, "facts do not exist, only interpretations,"[14] or as Derrida decreed, "there is nothing outside the text,"[15] or as Feyerabend's famous slogan has it, "Anything goes."[16] And if this conclusion appears morally too prickly and provocative, at most it may be mitigated by adding extrinsic, moderate notions and practices such as "dialogue," "conversation," "comprehension," "accommodation," "tolerance," "cooperation," "recognition," "inclusion," or even "appeal to the UN," or anything else that might serve to keep people from reverting to the wild, warlike state of nature.

But then it becomes impossible to build a liberal society, and if by chance we find that we have inherited one, it becomes impossible to maintain and defend it. What is so special about liberalism, if anything? What is it that makes liberal regimes so commendable, if indeed they are?

The development of the liberal philosopher John Gray's ideas may be considered emblematic and paradigmatic of the destiny and difficulties of liberalism as it grapples with value-pluralism, and also of its descending trajectory toward relativism. First, he believed confidently in a few liberal principles.[17] Then he concluded "that none of the four constitutive elements of doctrinal liberalism—universalism, individualism, egalitarianism, or meliorism—survives the ordeal by value-pluralism and that liberalism as a political philosophy is therefore dead."[18] In the end, he has been tempted to turn to the past. Faced with the eternal liberal problem of "how the diversity of individuals and communities in late modern societies can coexist in common institutions which they accept as legitimate,"[19] he has sought a modus vivendi by proposing this solution: "Liberal universalists claim that what they take to be liberal values are authoritative for every regime. Liberal relativists deny that there are any universal values. Both are mistaken. There are minimal standards of decency and legitimacy that apply to all contemporary regimes but they are not liberal values writ large."[20]

This would be nice to believe but it is incompatible with relativism. If, as relativists believe and Gray agrees, "there is no one resolution of conflicts among liberties that is everywhere right" and "no procedure for resolving such conflicts that is everywhere desirable," and moreover, if "each procedure can be defended in the context of particular traditions and historical circumstances,"[21] then the idea of "minimal standards" is without justification because it is clearly transcultural. On the contrary, if "all or nearly all ways of life have interests that make peaceful coexistence worth pursuing,"[22] and a modus vivendi is "impossible in a regime in which the varieties of the good are seen as symptoms of error or heresy,"[23] that is to say, in a regime that does not admit tolerance or respect, then it must be observed that tolerance and respect are typically liberal values. Therefore liberalism is not dead.

In short, if relativism is correct, liberalism errs with its claims to universal validity, its rights for all humanity, and its idea of producing a regime better than anyone else's. This would be ethnocentrism in disguise, just as Gray affirms. Liberalism is "the only sort of regime in which *we*—in our historical circumstance as late moderns—can live well."[24] The idea that liberal freedoms are good in themselves, that they reflect a given independent moral order, also finds no rational justification.[25] Alternatively, if a few principles do exist that have or should have value for all political regimes, then relativism is mistaken. Either "anything goes" for every regime, or there are "minimal standards of decency and legitimacy that apply to *all* contemporary regimes." That means, either relativism or liberalism. But even at the cost of appearing arrogantly ethnocentric, liberalism is a commendable regime also in the eyes of relativists. It is the regime in which they prefer to live. Thus there is a reason to believe that relativism is mistaken. And fortunately, it is.

If we examine it seriously, the view that any given culture is equal in value to any other is no less doubtful than the view that a given culture is better than others. If we cannot express the latter view because we are not permitted to say "better than," neither can we affirm the former because the expression "equal to" requires a *common* point of reference, which relativism does not allow us.

Moreover, the argument that adopting the relativist's point of view produces regimes that are more tolerant, democratic, open than others actually presupposes something denied by relativism itself: that tolerance and democracy and openness are values that should hold good for these other regimes as well. But if we seriously affirm that value judgments are all internal to a given culture, then we must conclude that each culture has its own, and has no way of appreciating or recommending those of others.

In the end, relativism is paralyzing. From its point of view, all that one can correctly express are judgments like "This is *my* regime" or "This is the regime in which *I* prefer to live." But how shall we respond to those who deny, oppose, or wish to destroy those regimes? Since everyone has his own values and his own criteria for values, and there is no external criterion to use for ranking them, the result would be the suspension of judgment and the lowering of defenses. Thus if we stick to relativism we will become mute or surrender with hands up.

That relativism is incompatible with liberalism is obvious. In any of its versions, liberalism is the doctrine of the fundamental rights of human beings as human beings, as they are recognized today by international charters. If we really want to, we can deny that these rights have a religious, primarily Christian foundation, but we cannot deny that they are based on a moral and metaphysical conception of human beings that is held to be *true,* and therefore they are *transcultural.* The liberal who asserts that man was born "endowed with certain inalienable rights" does not add "according to my opinion" or "according to my culture." He means to speak the truth; he means to say that this is *valid for everyone.* But if, for relativism, ethical truth does not exist and transcultural judgments cannot exist either, then relativism and liberalism are in conflict.

MULTICULTURALISM

What about multiculturalism, which is a political application of relativism today? Here too we must start with a well-established fact: modern societies are composed of minorities, communities, varied ethnic and cultural groups. Here too we find the same challenge: how to bind them together and govern them. Should we reduce this complexity to a unit and oblige everyone to respect a minimum code of values, or should we give free rein to diversities and let groups govern themselves? Should we affirm that there are criteria with which we may determine whether one culture is better or worse than another, or should we assert that no common measure exists and therefore all forms of culture are to be respected by all other cultures? Liberals take the former position; relativists the latter. Multiculturalism is the political doctrine and policy deriving from this second line of thinking. But it too is indefensible for both theoretical and practical reasons.

The theoretical reasons. Multiculturalism has two strong points, consisting of two arguments. The first is empirical: cultures confer identity upon individuals by giving them personality, a role, and self-awareness. One theorist of multiculturalism has written, "Culture shapes [men] in countless ways, forms them into certain kinds of persons, and cultivates certain attachments, affections, moral and psychological dispositions, taboos and modes of reasoning. Far from being purely formal and culturally neutral, their capacity for autonomy is structured in a particular way, functions within flexible but determinate limits and defines and assesses options in certain ways."[26] Therefore cultures are indispensable.

The second argument for multiculturalism is normative. As a liberal scholar leaning toward multiculturalism has noted, a good life requires that two preconditions be satisfied: "to lead our life from the inside, in accordance to our beliefs about what gives value to life," and "to be free to question those beliefs, to examine them in light of whatever information, examples, arguments our culture can provide."[27] The free society is one that not only "allows people to pursue their current way of life but also gives them access to information about other ways of life."[28] Therefore, "cultures are valuable not in and of themselves, but because it is only by having access to a societal culture that people have access to a range of meaningful options."[29] Thus, cultures are the bricks and mortar of freedom, and in order to protect this good, we must recognize the rights of cultures, which means the rights of groups.

Both arguments contain a grain of truth. It is true that cultures shape us, even though we should not exaggerate their importance in this regard, because it is the nature of human beings, of their critical, argumentative, and creative capacities, to transcend any culture in which they may be living. It is also true that the availability of more cultures allows us to make comparisons and express pondered and informed judgments on the type of good life we would like to pursue. The more we know, the richer we are inwardly. The greater our knowledge, the wider our horizons. As Popper remarked, "Had there been no Tower of Babel, we should invent it."[30] But we should not exaggerate the importance of this maxim, because even though we are nourished by the sheer abundance of data, we are also overwhelmed by it. This, ironically, is one of the reasons why Popper denied that scientific theories can be inferred inductively from the observation of established facts. We cannot carry out the command "Observe!" if we do not know what to observe (or at least have ideas about what is important to observe). The same goes for the command "Choose!"

However, although we may concede that multiculturalism has some reasonable starting points, we must note that the conclusions deriving from them are not as reasonable. From the fact that individuals cannot be what they are without a culture of reference, we may not deduce that that culture exists independently of those individuals, like a club that they join. And from the fact that having many cultural options is food for individual freedom, we may not deduce that cultures have the right to exist independently of the lifestyles they propose. It is illegitimate to infer that since minority groups exist in every society, and particularly in every complex society, we must therefore recognize group rights. A look at the contradictions that may arise between group rights and individual rights will help us see why.

Suppose that in a certain culture, parents are authorized to arrange marriages for their children without their consent. Or suppose that in a given culture, it is the norm for children to work, or for women to be subjected to genital mutilation. The problem is: must we respect that culture because it shapes the identity of its members and enriches our options, even if it violates their individual rights as defined in the wider society of which they are part; or must we censure that culture because it conflicts with fundamental rights, even though it provides the basis for that person's identity? Which should prevail: the rights of the individual or the rights of the group?

Liberals believe that the rights of the individual must prevail.[31] Moreover, from the liberal standpoint, cultures do not have an absolute right to exist, to survive, or to be protected. Such rights may be recognized in some cases but not in others. If a community of cannibals moves to New York, the mayor is not

required to recognize their right to pursue their dietary preferences (much less offer them a meal). If a community of shamans
moves in, no one can stop them from performing innocent cer-
emonies, say, to chase away the evil spirit of traffic or pollution.
To concede or not concede group rights depends on the kind
of rights requested and their conformity to fundamental rights
guaranteed to all citizens in the greater society. If the groups
respect fundamental rights, their customs will be allowed; if not,
they will be prohibited. In a liberal society, individuals come
first, not the society itself. Group rights do not exist, or they are
only secondary. For liberals, the rule holds that any violation of
basic rights *always* amounts to violence against human beings,
whereas the violating of group rights may *at times* safeguard
individual freedom.

A doctrine may be wrong yet still have useful effects. Galileo's mechanics, for example, is wrong, but we cannot do without it. The idea that all rights have their origin in a positive
constitution is also wrong, but it may induce virtuous behavior. Multiculturalism, on the other hand, is not only wrong but
harmful. The practical reasons for repudiating it are no less
important or less convincing than the theoretical reasons for
doing so.

The first drawback of multiculturalism is that it has planted
and fostered a guilt complex in many Europeans and other
Westerners. When minority groups of all types—ethnic, religious, or cultural—contest the majority of the greater society as
being hostile, insensitive to differences, or not open to alien customs and practices, the majority often gives way, backing down
from its position, as if ashamed, insecure, or remorseful. This is
why the West continually beats its breast and begs forgiveness.
It behaves like a parent afraid to be too strict, who surrenders to
his child's every whim, undermining his own parental authority

and influence, and not realizing how bad this is for the child. And for this self-flagellation, politically correct language provides the best whip.

The second drawback of multiculturalism is a consequence of the first. Once the majority society has chosen the path of concession, the minority groups slowly displace it. This results in a weakening of the collective identity and the flight of the traditional identity toward a different or indistinct one. The process begins with a crescendo of reasonable premises, ending in suicidal conclusions. Thus, once we have admitted that groups have the right to profess their own religion, we proceed to the idea that no religion must be subject to restriction. Next, we maintain that the religion of any given group is equal in value to that of any other group. In the end, we find ourselves concluding that the religion of the majority is an obstacle to the religions of the groups. Thus the greater society gives way under pressure because it feels it is in the wrong.

The third drawback of multiculturalism is the sum, at times tragic, of the previous two. Adopted as a policy for the integration of immigrants and as a measure against social conflict, multiculturalism is doing the exact opposite of what it was hoped to accomplish. Groups that have become accustomed to being respected collectively have put forward requests pertaining not only to religious worship, education, diet, and dress code, but also to more serious matters including marriage, relations between the sexes, and medical practices. With their generally low levels of education and slim economic opportunities, many groups of immigrants have concentrated themselves within limited spaces in peripheral areas, and often live in degrading conditions. This marginalization has been reinforced by the indifference of the political authorities, with their unspoken conviction that such ghettoes are more easily controlled, and by the guilty and secret intention to exploit the labor of immigrants (often like the new slaves). Some immigrant communities have become territorial enclaves within national boundaries and have begun to demand autonomy. The establishing of *shariah* courts in some parts of the UK is one illustration of this state of affairs, as are the social ghettoes burgeoning in all the major cities of Europe. There have been several emblematic examples of these perverse consequences.

In England, after the terrorist attack on London, Trevor Phillips, president of the Commission for Racial Equality, made a speech titled "Sleepwalking to Segregation." Adviser to the prime minister, and a left-wing politician, Phillips launched into a typical anathema against the United States: "This is a segregated society, in which the one truth that is self-evident is that people cannot and never will be equal. That is why, for all of us who care about racial equality and integration, America is not our dream, but our nightmare." Then he acknowledged that in England "we are in danger of throwing out the integrationist baby along with the assimilationist bathwater. In recent years we've focused far too much on the 'multi' and not enough on the common culture." In the end, he admitted, "here is where I think we are: we are sleepwalking our way to segregation. We are becoming strangers to each other and we are leaving communities to be marooned outside the mainstream."[32]

In the Netherlands, the results of multiculturalism haven't been any rosier. Pim Fortuyn, murdered by an Islamic fundamentalist on May 6, 2002, was a politically controversial figure, but was right on target when he wrote: "The West opts for a strategy that is only palliative. It tries to integrate Islamic countries in the economy of the capitalistic market and to maintain the best possible relations with them on a political and cultural level. It would be a correct strategy if it were not so scandalously partial and unilateral. It is unilateral because the West refuses to define its own culture. . . . A valid idea of a multicultural society should begin by defining the basic values of our own culture."[33]

But this is exactly the crucial point: "defining the basic values of our own culture" makes sense if we mean to appreciate them, defend them, and even judge them better than others. But relativists have taught us that we mustn't use the word "better," and the multiculturalists have put this teaching into practice. Unfortunately, the social reality of Europe and the West is seeking revenge against their theories and policies, harming us all.

INTEGRATION AND CONVERSION

There is a question to be raised here. If multiculturalism does not solve but rather exacerbates the problem of integrating immigrants because it weakens the identity of the greater society and if that identity in liberal Western society irrefutably springs from a Christian matrix, should we then ask immigrants to convert to Christianity? The answer is no, we cannot demand a *religious* conversion, but we can ask for a *civil* one.

Consider the situation in our liberal states. As I have already mentioned many times, typically they are founded on rights that are not legislatively constructed by those same states but have been recognized as natural. For this reason, these rights have been defined as "inalienable," "sacred," "intangible," "nonnegotiable," etc. Thus, the Universal Declaration of Human Rights (1948) speaks of the *"recognition* of the inherent dignity and of the equal and inalienable rights of all members of the human family." The Convention for the Protection of Human Rights and Fundamental Freedoms (1950) speaks of the *"recognition"* of those rights. The European Charter of Fundamental Rights (2000) states that "the Union *recognizes* the rights, freedoms, and principles set out hereafter," and the European Constitution (2004) affirms that "The Union shall *recognize* the rights, freedoms, and principles set out in the Charter of Fundamental Rights." Clearly, the verb "to recognize" means something different from "to concede," "to attribute," or "to emanate." To say that a state "recognizes" (or "safeguards" or "respects") fundamental rights means that those rights belong to its citizens *independently* of the action of that state, and *antecedently* to their condition as citizens. Exactly like the natural law of the liberal tradition.

It is to this law that Islamic immigrants (like everyone else) are asked to convert, not to the Christian religion, which first in Europe, then in the West, and then elsewhere has nurtured and justified that law. The immigrant, just like any native, is asked to swear his oath on a charter, not on the Bible. Even when the formula of that oath mentions the word "God," this does not entail any obligation to convert.[34] The immigrant is asked to become a *citizen,* not a *true believer.* It is up to him to translate the contents of that charter into the vocabulary of his culture of origin, or vice versa. He may have to repudiate parts of his culture that are in conflict with that charter (if there are any), reinterpret or update still others. This is not an act of despotism on the part of the greater society. The entire process seeks to satisfy mutual interests. By moving toward the greater society in which he seeks to be integrated, the immigrant will gain the advantage of being respected by its laws. By integrating him as a citizen, the greater society will gain the equal advantage of the immigrant's admission into that society.

This civil conversion is hardly an imposition of an authoritarian state, but a corollary of liberal principles. Here too, Kant may assist us in understanding why. "Hospitality," he claimed, "means the right of a stranger not to be treated with hostility when he arrives on someone else's territory."[35] It does *not* mean "the right of a guest to be entertained, for this would require a special friendly agreement whereby he might become a member of the native household for a certain time." Hospitality implies that hostile and aggressive treatment toward the stranger is prohibited; therefore it implies the *"right of resort,* for all men are entitled to present themselves in the society of others by virtue of their right to communal possession of the earth's surface. Since the earth is a globe, they cannot disperse over an infinite area, but must necessarily tolerate one another's company."[36] But if the right of resort exists because human beings cannot spread over an infinite area, this right cannot be unconditional, for neither can human beings gather in ever-growing concentrations. As a consequence, the right of hospitality does *not* amount to indiscriminate or indefinite allowance to a stranger to enter into another country. As Kant wrote, "this natural right of hospitality, i.e. the right of strangers, does not extend beyond those conditions which make it possible for them to *attempt* to enter into relations with the native inhabitants."[37]

The problem of Islamic integration in Europe has a theoretical solution as long as both sides are politically willing to find one and apply it. If this problem has not yet been solved, or if the solution has been unsatisfactory, the main reason lies in Europe's hesitation in recognizing its own traditional Christian law (which for Europe is actually secular constitutional law) and making others respect it. The feebleness of European identity, an effect of secularism and of widespread relativism, is detrimental both to the European hosts and to the immigrants knocking on their doors. If the tensions created by immigration have now been transferred to the plane of public safety and have come to be handled by judges, policemen, and armies, this means that the earlier measures of education, civil conversion, and transmission of European values have all failed. This also means that the European identity is so insecure, so unable to stand up for itself, so unattractive and lackluster that it stirs no positive response in immigrants, and at times elicits their outright rejection. If Europe is not a *melting pot* but only a container, this is because it does not have enough energy to melt down and fuse its contents.

This phenomenon, known as "culture shock" or "anxiety," has been investigated in great detail by many scholars.[38] Cardinal Ratzinger, examining the objections raised against the inclusion of references to Christianity in the preamble to the European Charter, asked,

> *Who would be offended by this? Whose identity is threatened thereby? The Muslims, who so often tend to be mentioned in this context, feel threatened, not by the foundations of our Christian morality, but by the cynicism of a secularized culture that denies its own foundations. Nor are our Jewish fellow citizens offended by the reference to the Christian roots of Europe, since these roots go back to Mount Sinai and bear the imprint of the voice that rang out on the mountain of God. We are united with the Jews in those great basic orientations given to man by the Ten Commandments. The same applies to the reference to God: it is not the mention of God that offends those who belong to other religions; rather it is the attempt to construct the human community in a manner that absolutely excludes God.[39]*

This Godless community—the experiment that Europe is conducting today with the help of secularism, scientism, relativism, and multiculturalism—is not only an impediment to building an identity, but also an obstacle to integration. When Europe's identity is weak, its own integration policies become ineffective or even counterproductive.

ISLAMIC FUNDAMENTALISM AND INTERRELIGIOUS DIALOGUE

Things aren't much better with respect to the problem of Islamic fundamentalism. Here too Europe's identity crisis has contributed to our failure to find a solution, and sometimes to our failure to understand just how serious a problem it is.

There is a risk of fundamentalism in all religions, especially monotheistic ones. If there is only one God, if there is only one source of salvation, one holy book containing the only truth, then the way is open for us to consider all other religions false, immature, or mythological, and to regard their followers as sinners, infidels, or apostates. To go from this point to seeing them as adversaries or enemies is a giant leap, but this can happen very quickly, and if it does, fundamentalism is often responsible. It interprets faith in a totalitarian and exclusive manner because it conceives religion as absorbing every aspect of life, and it is unwilling to recognize that other faiths may have similar value.

Christianity has been fundamentalist in some phases of its history, and there are still individuals and groups who follow the Christian faith in a fundamentalist way. But Christianity has developed various antidotes to this phenomenon. It has come to accept the principle of religious freedom and to distinguish between error and the person committing the error. It has withdrawn from the position of *instrumentum regni,* the crutch of states or political regimes. It has avoided identifying itself with any specific social order. It views theology, the science of God, as a science like any other, progressing and correcting itself in the face of challenges raised by new circumstances. Christianity has come to terms with modernity and has not shut itself off.

But Christianity's best antidote against fundamentalism is Christianity itself. Jesus Christ's message is one of *love:* "These things I command ye, that ye love one another." (John 15:17) "By this shall all men know that ye are my disciples, if ye have love one to another." (John 13:35) "Love your enemies . . . pray for them who persecute you." (Matthew 5:44; Luke 6:35) It is a message of *brotherhood:* "For one is your master, even Christ, and ye are all brethren." (Matthew 23:8) Of *charity:* "Give to him that asketh thee and from him that would borrow of thee turn not thou away." (Matthew 5:42) Of *benevolence:* "whatsoever ye would that men should do to you, do ye even so to them." (Matthew 7:12) Of *harmony:* "Blessed are the peacemakers." (Matthew 5:9) The instruments of Jesus Christ and of every Christian for the dissemination of this message are the preaching of sermons, the fulfilling of missions, the act of witnessing, and even the acceptance of persecution and martyrdom. The aim of the Christian message is the "kingdom of heaven," not a political revolution or a social order on earth. Jesus Christ did not leave us a political doctrine, even though Christians may find useful suggestions for politics in His teachings.[40]

Has Islam rejected fundamentalism as Christianity has done?

Not with regard to the origins and dissemination of the Islamic religion. The Christ is a master who leads huge crowds; the prophet of Allah is a commander of armies. The former uses words and sermons; the latter keeps a sword at his side. One founded a church; the other, a state or political community. From its earliest beginnings, the history of Islam has been a story of military campaigns and wars, conquest and persecution. This history undeniably shows elements of fundamentalism.

Nor with regard to the holy scripture of Islam. The Gospel is the *story* of the life of Jesus, his teachings and his actions. It serves as a guide for every Christian to understand how to find salvation. The Koran was *dictated* by Allah. It serves not only as a book of meditation and prayer, and more precisely, of *submission,* but also as a detailed guide to behavior in daily life, for family, civil, community, and political concerns. There are as many rules for earthly life as there are commandments for attaining paradise. And the call to arms is as frequently mentioned as the preaching of sermons.

Does this mean that Islam is in itself fundamentalist and violent? It does mean that this question is a legitimate and pertinent one, to be asked without preconceptions, unencumbered by the hypocrisy of politically correct language. But conflicting answers are given in response.

At one extreme, we find answers like this: "In Islam, violence is more than the expression of a brutal force. It is the embodiment and the proof of an absolute force, attributed to Allah."[41] There are indeed many violent passages in the Koran, alongside references to revenge, chastisement, punishment, threats, curses, and murder to be carried out against anyone who does not believe in Allah. For example: "And slay them wherever ye find them, and drive them out of the places whence they drove you out, for persecution is worse than slaughter." (II:191) "If they turn back (to enmity) then take them and kill them wherever ye find them, and choose no friend nor helper from among them." (IV:89) "I will throw fear into the hearts of those who disbelieve. Then smite the necks and smite of them each finger." (VIII:12) "And fight them until persecution is no more, and religion is all for Allah." (VIII:39) "Slay the idolaters wherever ye find them, and take them (captive) and besiege them and prepare for them each ambush." (IX:5) "Fight against such of those who have been given the Scripture as believe not in Allah nor the Last Day, and forbid not that which Allah hath forbidden by His messenger, and follow not the religion of truth, until they pay the tribute readily, being brought low." (IX:29) And so on.

At the other extreme, we find a completely different answer: "Islam, like all world religions, neither supports nor requires illegitimate violence," and "Islam, from the Koran to Islamic law, does not permit terrorism and places limits on the use of violence."[42] There is textual evidence in the Koran also for this view. For example: "Those who believe (in that which is revealed unto thee, Muhammad) and those who are Jews, and Christians, and Sabaeans—whoever believeth in Allah and the Last Day—surely their reward is with their Lord, and there shall no fear come upon them neither shall they grieve." (II:62) "There is no compulsion in religion. The right direction is henceforth distinct from error." (II:256) "For that cause We decreed for the Children of Israel that whosoever killeth a human being for other than manslaughter or corruption in the earth, it shall be as if he had killed all mankind, and whoso saveth the life of one, it shall be as if he had saved the life of mankind." (V:32) "And if thy Lord willed, all who are in the earth would have believed together. Wouldst thou (Muhammad) compel men until they are believers?" (X:100) "It is the truth from the Lord of you (all). Then whosoever will, let him believe, and whosoever will, let him disbelieve." (XVIII:30) "And I shall not worship that which ye worship. Nor will ye worship that which I worship. Unto you your religion, and unto me my religion." (CIX:4–6)

If there is a conclusion to be drawn from these conflicting passages, it is that the *wording* of scripture alone does not determine the spirit and *interpretation* of its text. While the wording is certainly not irrelevant, its interpretation is vital because this determines not only the way in which the wording is understood, but also the way in which it is experienced and practiced. Since the fundamentalist approach to any religion depends more on scriptural interpretation than on the text itself, the question we must ask Islam today is: does it allow for nonfundamentalist interpretations that can coexist with nonfundamentalist interpretations of other religions, both within a society and internationally? Can Islam find a way to coexist with Christianity and Judaism?

As early as *Nostra Aetate* of the Second Vatican Council, the Catholic Church's answer was interreligious dialogue. But this approach is doomed from the very outset. How can there be an authentic interreligious dialogue if monotheistic and revealed religions are holistic systems, each with its own truth and its own criteria for ascertaining truth? If the believer of one religion cannot admit the truth of another? He who says *I am the truth* excludes anyone else from making the same claim. In the strictest and most technical sense, dialogue presupposes precisely the opposite: that the interlocutors be open to revision and to the rejection of the truth with which they began their dialectical exchange. As Popper put it, the principle of dialogue is: "I may be wrong and you may be right, but by an effort we may get nearer to the truth."[43] Dialogue has no meaning if at the outset both say: "This is *the truth* and I will never change my mind." In such a case, at most, their encounter may be an exchange of information, useful for learning about each other but unable to produce agreements on substantial issues. Commonly shared but terribly ambiguous formulas, such as "the sons of Abraham," "There is but one God," "God is truth," are of no help. As has been noted, "To declare that we are all the sons of Abraham logically has no meaning. Rather, we need to know who among the Jews, Muslims, and Christians carry out the works of Abraham, which all tend toward an absolute, unwavering faith in the revealed God. . . . It is actions, not gene-alogy, that make a man the son of Abraham."[44]

In his celebrated Regensburg lecture of September 2006, Benedict XVI returned to this issue and reformulated the question. Speaking on the relationship between faith and reason, he referred to the Islamic concept of *jihad,* or "holy war," and quoted the words of the Byzantine emperor Manuel II Palaeolo-gus, "God is not pleased by blood, and not acting reasonably is contrary to God's nature."[45] Then the pope posed the problem: "Is the conviction that acting unreasonably contradicts God's nature merely a Greek idea, or is it always and intrinsically true?"[46] From such a point of view, the question we need to ask Islam becomes: Is the God of Islam a God of reason or a God of the sword?

In response, thirty-eight Islamic scholars signed a reassuring and promising letter addressed to the pope in October 2006. A subsequent letter, one year later, was signed by a hundred thirty-eight Islamic authorities, clerics, and intellectuals.[47] The writ-ers affirm that Islam is a religion of peace, and they cite Surah II:256 (which the pope had indeed mentioned): "There is no compulsion in religion." Next they explain that in the Islamic view, the transcendent nature of God does not preclude a human relationship with Him. Then they define *jihad* as a "struggle in the way of God," and state that "as a *political* entity Islam spread partly as a result of conquest, but the greater part of its expansion came as a result of preaching and missionary activ-ity." The Islamic authorities conclude with their main thesis, that "the *Two Greatest Commandments* are an area of common ground and a link between the Qur'an, the Torah and the New Testament."

In Islam, the first of these two commandments is: "There is no god but God, He Alone, He hath no associate, His is the sovereignty and His is the praise and He hath power over all things." (Hadith 3934) The second is: "It is not righteousness that ye turn your faces to the East and the West, but righteous is he who believeth in God and the Last Day and the angels and the Scripture and the prophets; and giveth wealth, for love of Him, to kinsfolk and to orphans and the needy and the way-farer and to those who ask, and to set slaves free; and observeth proper worship and payeth the poor-due. And those who keep their treaty when they make one, and the patient in tribulation and adversity and time of stress. Such are they who are sincere. Such are the pious." (Surah II:177)

In Christianity, the first of the greatest commandments is: "Love the Lord your God with all your heart and soul, mind and strength." The second one is: "Love your neighbor as your-self." (Matthew 22:37–39; Mark 12:30–31)

The effort to close the distance and reach a mutual under-standing expressed in those letters was decidedly new and com-mendable, as was the acknowledgment that "the relationship between these two religious communities [is] the most important factor in contributing to meaningful peace around the world. If Muslims and Christians are not at peace, the world cannot be at peace." But the cause of interreligious dialogue has not been enhanced by this effort; on the contrary, it has been weakened. If the correspondence between these two great commandments truly had essential religious consequences—as it should have if the common ground were truly a religious one ("the common essentials of our two religions"), and if the dialogue were truly an interreligious one ("let this common ground be the basis of all future interreligious dialogue between us"), then Christian-ity and Islam would have to be the same religion expressed in different words, and the God of Christians and the God of Mus-lims would be different manifestations of the same God. At that point, the whole dispute would be reduced to normal questions of interpretation within a single religious archetype. It would be a peripheral dispute concerning details.

But it *isn't* that way. Those same one hundred thirty-eight scholars affirmed that "Islam and Christianity are obviously different religions." And it is equally obvious that the Christians are of the same opinion. Prince Ghazi bin Muhammad bin Talal of Jordan, in a letter to the Vatican secretary of state, affirmed, "We consider complete theological agreement between Christians and Muslims inherently not possible by definition." And with equal forcefulness, the Christians agree. Therefore, on the religious level there is no "common ground." Interreligious dialogue is simply impossible. Such a dialogue could produce but one result: either a *friendly conversation* based on mutual good will, or a *verbal adjustment* based on linguistic ambiguities, or a form of *syncretism*.[48] No theologian could defend it and the believers of both religions would reject it.

Is there no other way to "keep peace in the world"? Must we resign ourselves to a never-ending tug of war? In his Regensburg lecture and elsewhere on other important occasions, Benedict XVI rejected such resignation and suggested an answer. Rather than speak of interreligious dialogue, he proposed an *intercultural dialogue,* or more precisely, a "dialogue of cultures."[49] In my view, the difference between the two is fundamental and merits closer inquiry. An analogy between scientific and religious systems will shed light on the problem.

Scientific theories consist of three main elements: an axiomatic core, principles of inference, and consequences expressed in empirically testable terms. For example, in Copernican theory those consequences are a certain movement of the planets; in Newtonian theory, the acceleration of a body in free fall under the influence of gravity; in the wave theory of light, a certain reflection of light rays. Two divergent theories may be compared on the common ground of their empirical results, and one may be judged better than the other. By "better" we mean that it has greater empirical content (that is, verified results), more predictive power (testable expectations), more heuristic capacity (suggesting new lines of research), and so on.

Analogously, religious systems also consist of three components: a dogmatic core, a set of principles of interpretation, and an indefinite number of cultural (especially ethical) consequences, such as certain rights attributed or denied to human beings, certain social customs that are permitted or prohibited, certain forms of interpersonal relations that are allowed or censured, certain political institutions that are recommended or banned. Two religious systems may be compared by their cultural consequences, and here too one may be judged better than the other. By "better, " we mean that it recognizes and respects more fundamental rights, satisfies more expectations, allows for more efficient, transparent, democratic institutions, and so on. This cultural comparison, which is an authentic intellectual, political, and social competition, has no direct impact on the original religious premises. Unlike what occurs in scientific domains, where the observation of a negative consequence of a theory falsifies it, in religious domains an undesired cultural consequence does not confute a faith in a technical sense, but at most induces or obliges its followers to reinterpret its dogmatic core. A cultural comparison is more indirect than a scientific one. And it is certainly less ambitious: it does not decide which of the two religions is "true" or "false," but which one produces better or worse cultural consequences. In this, however, it is efficacious. An intercultural comparison, unlike an interreligious one, is an authentic *debate* during which, following the logic proper to *dialectical exchange,*[50] the two sides may revise their initial opinions, correct them, integrate them, or even reject them. Whether such cultural debate brings about a revision of the religious core to which the cultures in question are linked or from which they stem is an open question. If a revision does occur, it leads to religious conversion. Even if it doesn't, a genuine discussion has taken place.

Our analogy is illuminating also for another reason. Scientists have at their disposal an *empirical stock* of data, observations, measurements, experiments, protocols, low-level generalizations. This is the common ground of their dialogue, the touchstone with which they evaluate their hypotheses. Analogously, groups of people develop social, economic, and political relationships, which generate needs, then demands, then rights (for example: the right to life, dignity, respect; freedom of expression and political liberties). As they are broadened and secured, these rights come to be considered so fundamental that they are enshrined in international charters and treaties. This is a *moral stock* of values, a common ground on which people may evaluate their own ways of life and conceptions of the good.

For the purposes of dialogue, our question now is not "Is Islam compatible with Christianity and Judaism?" or even "Is Islam a religion of reason or of the sword?" but rather "Are the cultural consequences deriving from Islam *compatible* with the moral stock of universal values? With democracy? With the charters of human rights?"

That this is indeed the appropriate ground of comparison is confirmed by the one hundred thirty-eight Islamic scholars where they quote the only surah of the Koran that clearly suggests as much: "Had God willed He could have made you one community. But that He may try you by that which He hath given you (He hath made you as ye are). So vie one with another in good works. Unto God ye will all return, and He will then inform you of that wherein ye differ." (V:48) We learn several things from these words: that religious diversity is not contrary to the will of Allah, that Allah tests those who are divided, and—the most important point—that the test consists of a competition in "good works." Therefore, dialogue cannot be conducted on the basis of the truth of Allah's words, but on the consequences that Muslims derive from them, and on the works they perform by following them. This is not an interreligious dialogue, but an intercultural one. Its object is not, say, the Trinity or transubstantiation, but rather equality, freedom, tolerance, and the like.

Unfortunately, it is precisely on this common ground of "good works" that we must conclude *today* that Islam loses by comparison.

In the world of Islam, the moral stock of universal values is scarcely honored. There is little if any respect for religious freedom, sexual equality, dignity of the individual, freedom to choose one's marriage partner, freedom to criticize religion, tolerance, or the use of noncoercive means of persuasion. Violence is not unequivocally forbidden, and there are no clear-cut distinctions between the Koran and political power, between the state and civil society. Nor are there any authorities within Islamic society who have the power to issue official, binding interpretations in order to correct practices that may violate the universal values of humanity. It could be objected—and the one hundred thirty-eight sages do so in their letter—that this applies to the world of Islamic *politics* and not to that of religion. But that is indeed the point: once we have concluded that dialogue is between cultures and not between religions, it is precisely the political and social world of Islam, and the way religion shapes that world or demands it to be, that provides the crucial test. The courtesy and respect we owe the courageous and noble

Islamic interlocutors and scholars cannot keep us from concluding that Islam today has not passed this test. Like all judgments on historical phenomena, this verdict may be corrected in light of new events. However, at the present time, it is a well-founded judgment.

Of course Europe knows this, but refuses to admit it and doesn't like to talk about it. There is a profound reason why, which I have discussed at length. In Europe itself the moral stock of universal values has been called into question. Europe loves Islam for the same reason Islam hates Europe: because of Europe's secularism, relativism, multiculturalism, and its discrediting of religious feeling. Europe offers a dialogue to Islam for the same reason it does not want to talk to itself: the rejection of its own roots.[51] In such conditions, everything is turned upside down: understanding Islam means collusion; union means adhesion; appreciation means submission. And the integration of Muslims means surrendering to them.

Europe and the entire West are well aware of this but are like patients resigned to their disease. That proud and powerful liberal doctrine that Europeans invented is now in a phase of cultural demise, and those influential liberal regimes they built and exported all over the globe are now at the lowest point in a downward trajectory. The liberal European state and liberal European society are paying the consequences. This will be the last topic I examine before my conclusion.

THE EXPROPRIATION OF MORALS

There is an optimistic philosophy of history that goes like this: At the beginning of the modern era, the liberal state was born. Next came the democratic state, and then the welfare state. Each step forward brought an increase of freedom. But experience, purged of philosophy, tells a different story: At the beginning the state was liberal, then paternalistic, and finally totalitarian. Each step forward brought a diminishing of freedom. There is reason to believe and to worry that the second story is the true one.

Let us begin by observing that the modern state, any modern Western state, as we have said from the beginning, is a *hybrid* with two faces. One is the face of liberty and fundamental, inviolable rights; the other is the face of democracy and social rights. Using the well-known terminology of Isaiah Berlin,[52] we may say that our states intend to wed positive liberty or "freedom *to*" (the classical civil and political liberties) with negative liberty or "freedom *from*" (from poverty, ignorance, social constrictions, and so on). Or to use the terminology now in vogue, we might say that our states wish to wed freedom with social justice.

To this strange combination, Benedetto Croce gave the name of *hircocervus,* a mythical beast born of the unlikely union of two notions that cannot be combined because they belong to two very different categories: freedom, a "pure concept" referring to the Spirit's eternal mode of being; and social justice, an "empirical pseudo-concept" referring to a contingent mode of being in social relations. Even if we reject Croce's idealistic philosophy of freedom, which I have done in the first chapter, by bringing freedom back to its proper political ground, that of rights and institutions, the fact remains that the combination of the rights of freedom with the rights of social justice is now generating a form of state that is, to say the least, no less deformed and disturbing than Croce's mythical beast.

The two parts of this hybrid do not go together. Freedom tends in one direction; justice another. One produces inequality; the other promotes equality. One regards inequality as a natural condition and exalts the autonomy of individuals (to undertake initiatives, educate themselves, promote themselves), which inevitably renders them unequal. The other instead sees equality as natural and puts restraints on individual freedom (economic, social, fiscal) so that all are rendered equal. From the conflict between these two tendencies, the liberal state emerges transformed. Now also required to create the material conditions that foster equality and not merely limit itself to the political and juridical conditions in which freedom is exercised, the state is forced to change its nature. Since its new functions must all strive to protect, promote, and care for its citizens, like a good father with his children, it becomes a *paternalistic state.*

As has often been observed, the paternalistic state erases the distinction between state and civil society that is proper to the liberal state: if the state must correct inequalities or "injustices," then it cannot limit itself to the role of arbiter, ensuring that general rules are respected for the benefit of all. Rather, it must become an actor, producing special rules that give advantage to some of its supposedly disadvantaged citizens. This paternalistic intention may seem praiseworthy, but its own logic turns against it. The reason may be expressed in an intuitive formula: the more the state increases freedom "from," the more its intervention diminishes freedom "to." It's well known that Marxists tried to escape this conundrum by putting all production and redistribution of wealth into the hands of the state, thinking that total liberty and justice would have resulted; but as history has shown, this idea produces nothing but total slavery.

The risks that paternalism poses to freedom go beyond the continual creation of new social inequalities, however. Although the paternalistic state first concerns itself with economic inequalities, once the autonomy of society has been invaded, the state by inherent logic, not by fatal accident or evil intentions, is forced to go further and to concern itself with other social issues pertaining to civil society. Men do not live by bread alone, nor can equality be created only by spending generous sums of money. The demands for justice and protection are many. Once citizens have obtained a house, next they want a better neighborhood. Those who have state health coverage next want an improved quality of life. Those who have obtained an education next want better qualifications and then a career with a good salary, and then permanent employment. And so on. This spontaneous burgeoning of needs and the state's parallel intervention to satisfy them cause the demands for ever-new "rights" to keep multiplying within the paternalistic state.

Nor is this expansion of rights limited to the social needs of life. New kinds of demands begin to crop up. For example, if I have the right to marry whom I please, I also have the right to have a family. If I have the right to have a family, then I also have the right to have children, and if I have the right to procreate, why shouldn't I have the right to select healthy children? Thus, spontaneously but fatally, we slip into the sphere of ethics. And once we have entered there, we will find it hard to restrain our demands, just as we did in the sphere of economics. Thanks to science and technology, things are possible today that we could never have dreamed of in the past, so new desires and demands for further rights arise in response to the availability of these new options.

Like the liberal state, the paternalistic state must bow down to this reality. And so it does. Under the constant pressure of new demands for "liberty," "justice," or "equality," diverse functions concerning matters once relegated to "the community"—that is, once the province of families, neighborhoods, social and religious organizations—are now attributed to the state. A case in point is the issue of bioethics, which has now become a concern of the state, a new "good" regulated and distributed by public legislation.

This further expansion of the paternalistic state is much more destructive than the previous one. Rather than a broadening of its sphere of action, it is an authentic degeneration.[53] The state no longer decides only issues of social equality, it now decides what is *morally good* in matters of birth, marriage, quality of life, dignity of individuals and of embryos, death, and sex. The typical slogan of the paternalistic state, "from the cradle to the grave," turns out to be literally true. It is now up to the state to decide who is allowed to enter the cradle and to determine when and how we descend into the grave. The liberal state was only a guardian and custodian, but the paternalistic state has first become distributor and dispenser of benefits, then master of virtue.

Thus the paternalistic state *expropriates morality.* Called upon to decide what is good or bad for its citizens, it is forced to adopt its own moral vision, to sanction it by laws and establish punishments for those who infringe it. In the first chapter, we remarked how such a state, even though it loves to consider itself secular, is really not so at all because the moral vision it must assume in order to answer its citizens' demands renders it neither neutral nor indifferent toward *all* conceptions of the good. It must accept *one,* perhaps one at a time. Here we see that the state undergoes another transformation. Since it must concern itself with *all* aspects of life, the paternalistic state becomes an *ethically totalitarian state.*[54]

Christopher Dawson foresaw this development at its very outset, saying,

> *For the modern state, whether it is democratic, as it is in the United States or communistic as in the U.S.S.R., or*

Fascist as in pre-war Italy and Germany, or nationalistic as in the new states of Asia and Africa, is no longer content to confine itself to certain limited functions like the liberal state of the nineteenth century. In fact all modern states are totalitarian in so far as they seek to embrace the spheres of economics and culture, as well as politics in the strict sense of the word. They are concerned not merely with the maintenance of the public order and the defense of the people against external enemies. They have taken on responsibility for all the different forms of communal activity which were formerly left to the individual or to independent social organizations such as the churches, and they watch over the welfare of their citizens from the cradle to the grave.[55]

Note that in this last transformation of the state, no violence has occurred. The ethically totalitarian state is founded on the consensus, or rather on the widespread, ever-increasing demands of its citizens. To use a celebrated expression, it has become a "totalitarian democracy."[56] It is the citizens who ask the state to satisfy their new needs, who bring new cases of "injustice" to its attention and who beg it to provide them with new opportunities. Here secularism, relativism, and multiculturalism heat up to an explosive mixture. Since there is no longer a *single shared vision* of what is true, good, or right, and no *single, shared understanding* of limits or of sin, then there is no natural limit to citizens' demands or to the state's expropriation of morality. The outcome was clearly foreseen by John Paul II in the encyclical *Centesimus Annus* (46): "If there is no ultimate truth to guide and direct political activity, then ideas and convictions can easily be manipulated for reasons of power. As history demonstrates, a democracy without values easily turns into open or thinly disguised totalitarianism."

This totalitarianism is devious in many ways. For one thing, it asserts itself by respecting the best of rules. When the state is called upon to decide on ethical questions, its legislators do what they must do when faced with any question: they discuss the issue and take a vote. The ethically totalitarian state is democratic.

Furthermore, this totalitarianism is devious because it insinuates itself so naturally. Demanding ever-new rights, society turns to the state with requests such as "My group and I want this particular freedom. What harm will it do if we ask that it be granted to us alone, and if we do not impose it on anyone else?" Or this: "My group and I have this tendency or characteristic or desire. What harm would it do if we asked for special juridical recognition?" Questions like these spread and multiply, magnified by powerful propaganda, and a doubt slowly worms its way into society and dissolves. After all, why not? Why shouldn't I concede to another person something that I do not accept? Perhaps because my conception of the good is better than anyone else's? No, since we are relativists we cannot establish this, and in any case we cannot say it. So let the state create rights and decide what is good and issue its commandments and prohibitions. Or more precisely, not the state, but the parliamentary majority. Thus the most bizarre paradoxes arise. For example, the state is strict about wearing seat belts while driving, but indulgent concerning euthanasia. It is obliged to protect the health of its citizens, but free to decide on whether they live or die. It is attentive to questions of burial, but willing to anticipate it. It is concerned about its citizens' diet and food quality, but tolerant of "moderate quantities" of drugs. It is willing to recognize the rights of animals, but complacent with those who violate human rights. And so on, down to the most conclusive and absurd paradox: the state is tolerant of fundamentalist Islamic culture, but aggressive toward the principles of Christian believers.

And that's not all. With the paternalistic state, the hybrid (or *hircocervus*) loses its liberal face. With the ethically totalitarian state, the democratic face triumphs. But we come to a point where democracy also yields and the expropriators find themselves expropriated. More and more frequently it happens that laws are made not by representative legislative bodies following the procedures of public debate and popular control, but by organisms that are not made up of representatives chosen by the people, or to which other functions have been delegated. This phenomenon is far worse than the legislative production of law proper to democracy: it is the bureaucratic and technocratic production of juridical norms carried out by inappropriate means such as verdicts, sentences, white papers, treaties. It is the tombstone of the liberal state. Parliaments are actually being replaced today by "independent authorities," like central banks, labor unions, guilds and associations, and other organizations empowered to make decisions that affect everyone. And while the European Parliament or the Council of Europe or the supranational institutions in general intrude upon the autonomy of the democratic national parliaments without actually being democratic themselves, the high courts and constitutional courts step in to occupy what little space is left in the autonomy and sovereignty of citizens. As liberalism crumbles and paternalism spreads, these bureaucratic organisms are turning into authentic despots, superior to democratic powers. The bench and high courts, in order to enhance their own influence and transform themselves into an absolute authority, have even come up with a theory, never before contemplated by the liberal juridical or democratic traditions, according to which the task of judges is not to interpret and apply specific laws but to enforce general principles.

There have been many celebrated cases, often headline-makers, and there are more and more each day. It was not a decision of the British people or their Parliament that authorized tribunals of the *shariah* in UK territory, but an agreement made with Islamic groups. It was not a law of the United States Congress that first liberalized abortion in America, but a ruling of the Supreme Court. The Italian parliament has never authorized euthanasia, but court rulings have. No public debate preceded a court decision in the Netherlands that euthanasia may be performed on twelve-year-old children. Not by parliamentary law was same-sex marriage first granted equal status to marriage between a man and a woman in some countries. Not by parliamentary vote has eugenics become a right. No parliamentary decisions allow for polygamy to be freely practiced, as often occurs, or for the recognition of transgender rights. Nor is it the will of the people that distinctions be made between terrorists and "resistance fighters" who plot to carry out massacres, or that migrants be allowed to remain in a country they have entered illegally.

This "judicial imperialism,"[57] or "judicial universalism"[58] according to current definitions, acts exactly like a dictatorship: it imposes, orders, commands, speaking for everyone but not required to answer to anyone. Like all dictatorships, it makes a show of being inspired by a civil mission. Like all dictatorships, it believes itself to be enlightened, knowledgeable, and wise. And like all dictatorships, it claims to act in the name of the "common" good, of the "true" good, or the "sovereign" good.

In reality, like all dictatorships, it is the expression of ideologies or power groups.

THE DESCENDING TRAJECTORY
OF PUBLIC LIBERAL ETHICS

The main questions of bioethics (artificial procreation, abortion, euthanasia, assisted suicide), sexual ethics (homosexuality, gender identity), ethics of family relationships (nuclear families, marriage), the ethics of medical intervention and scientific research (embryonic experimentation, genetic engineering) are an excellent testing ground to see just how tightly the dictatorship of the ethically totalitarian state holds us in its grip. In this regard, liberalism has traveled down a descending trajectory that I will first describe before stating my own position.

I will put Kant and his law of morality at the starting point of this trajectory. In the second formula of his categorical imperative he states: "So act that you use humanity, whether in your own person or in the person of any other, always at the same time as an end, never merely as a means."[59] This law expresses a principle of autonomy, not in the sense that everyone is free to choose any orientation in life he desires, but in the sense that practical reason dictates to the will that law to which its choices must conform. That law is a rationalized version of a Christian commandment. Rationalized because, as Kant came to admit, "consciousness of this fundamental law may be called a fact of reason,"[60] and Christian because Kant did not intend to formulate a new morality but to bring traditional morality before the tribunal of practical reason (as he had brought Newtonian physics before the tribunal of pure reason). From his moral law, Kant drew consequences for public ethics. If a human being is always a person and never merely a means, then certain prohibitions must derive therefrom.

Infanticide (including abortion) is illicit. Parents "cannot destroy their child as if he were something they had made (since a being endowed with freedom cannot be a product of this kind)."[61] Polygamy is excluded because "the person who surrenders herself gains only part of the man who gets her completely, and therefore makes herself more into a thing."[62] Cohabitation, or as Kant called it, "concubinage,"[63] is equally excluded because in this case a woman "would be surrendering herself as a thing to the other's choice."[64] For the same reasons, prostitution,[65] homosexuality,[66] and suicide[67] are also excluded.

Without further elaboration, we may summarize Kant's ethical view in two points:

a) The law of morality is the (Christian) law of the categorical imperative, with which reason commands the will in a universal way.

b) The law of morality imposes *respect for the human person.*

Let us now examine another point in the descending trajectory of liberal ethics and look at a very different liberal thinker, John Stuart Mill. His main difference from Kant can be summed up in a single word: ethics has become *secular* instead of Christian. For Mill, God does not exist; or if He does, He operates in the private sphere without performing any appreciable public role. Mill acknowledges that "some of the precepts of Christ as exhibited in the Gospels—rising far above the Paulism which is the foundation of ordinary Christianity—carry some kinds of moral goodness to a greater height than had ever been attained before." These, however, serve as a scale that may be set aside after fulfilling its function. "But this benefit, whatever it amounts to, has been gained. Mankind have entered into the possession of it. It has become the property of humanity and cannot now be lost by anything short of a return to primeval barbarism."[68]

Once we have dispensed with God, or with any rationalized form of God, the individual decides for himself what is good for him by observing the consequences (overall or average) of his actions or his rules of action. This is the principle of utilitarianism. "I regard utility as the ultimate appeal on all ethical questions; but it must be utility in the largest sense, grounded on the permanent interests of man as a progressive being."[69] This is also a principle of autonomy, but is different from Kant's. For Kant, autonomy means obeying *the* universal, moral law. For Mill, autonomy means giving ourselves any compatible maxim of individual preferences: everyone must be free to pursue his own concept of happiness within the public limits of respect for the freedom of others to do the same, but with the private prerogative of being master of himself, without others being able to interfere with his own autonomy. In Mill's celebrated formulation, "the sole end for which mankind are warranted, individually and collectively, in interfering with the liberty of action of any of their number, is self-protection. . . . That the only purpose for which power can be rightfully exercised over any member of a civilized community, against his will, is to prevent harm to others. His own good, either physical or moral, is not a sufficient warrant. . . . Over himself, over his own body and mind, the individual is sovereign."[70] This means that as far as concerns the private sphere, which is "the appropriate region of human liberty,"[71] "the principle requires liberty of tastes and pursuits; of framing the plan of our life to suit our own character; of doing as we like, subject to such consequences as may follow: without impediment from our fellow creatures, so long as what we do does not harm them, even though they should think our conduct foolish, perverse, or wrong."[72]

Guided by this principle, public ethics changes its perspective on almost all major themes. Polygamy is allowed because even if it is "a mere riveting of the chains of one-half of the community, and an emancipation of the other from reciprocity of obligation towards them," it must be remembered that "this relation is as much voluntary on the part of the women concerned in it." In any case, Mill continues, moving from pluralism to multiculturalism, "I am not aware that any community has a right to force another to be civilized."[73] The use of drugs and toxic substances is also allowed: limits imposed by the state must be solely "for the prevention of crime, or of accident."[74] Moreover, "fornication must be tolerated and so must gambling."[75] Exposing oneself to life-threatening danger is also tolerated: "when there is not a certainty, but only a danger of mischief, no one but the person himself can judge of the sufficiency of the motive which may prompt him to incur the risk."[76] However, the freedom of pimps and keepers of gambling houses is uncertain because "the case is one of those which lie on the exact boundary line between two principles." Divorce is uncertain as well because marriage "has placed third parties in [a] peculiar position" and "has even called third parties into existence."[77] Nothing is said about suicide, but it is logical to assume it is allowed. If I have sovereignty over myself and if by the act of suicide I harm no one but myself, why should I not be allowed to put an end to my days?

Without going into great detail, we may sum up Mill's ethics in two points:

a) The law of morality is the (utilitarian) law that commands, as the best action (or rule of action), the one from which the greatest happiness for all ensues.

b) The law of morality imposes *respect for personal freedom.*

In comparison with Kant's view, the content of the moral law has changed. Mill, as he himself explains, is concerned not with "the so-called Liberty of the Will, so unfortunately opposed to the misnamed doctrine of Philosophical Necessity; but Civil, or Social Liberty: the nature and limits of the power which can be legitimately exercised by society over the individual."[78] His moral principle is clearly limited to and depends on the liberal society and state of his own time and place. It does not apply universally to all because, Mill claims, with Europe in mind, "Liberty, as a principle, has no application to any state of things anterior to the time when mankind have become capable of being improved by free and equal discussion."[79] Mill's moral law commands Mill's liberal man.

Let us take another point on the descending trajectory of liberal ethics and consider our own times. Mill, like Tocqueville, feared the dictatorship of the majority and the uniformity of individuals, which he called "the Chinese ideal of making all people alike." He asked, "What is it that has hitherto preserved Europe from this lot?" His answer was "the remarkable diversity of character and culture."[80] But such a fate has become inexorable today, furthered by those very factors that Mill pointed out: democracy, education, the expansion of trade and industrial manufacturing, and especially conformism.[81] Mill's prophecy has proved to be correct. Europe, even if not politically unified, is becoming more and more homogeneous in its customs, its lifestyle, and its ways of thinking. Paradoxically, such uniformity is due to the victory of Mill's principle: over themselves, over their bodies and minds, Europeans nowadays enjoy greater and greater sovereignty. God has vanished, the free choices of individuals come first, communities demand to maintain their own cultures and groups demand their rights. This is the true "unity in diversity," the triumph of the Millian man, the Millian woman, and especially of the Millian mother who claims "My body is mine and I control it."[82] There is yet another paradox: the very state against whose intervention Mill protested, proclaiming the sacredness of the private "sphere of action," has now become, on request, the invader of this sphere and the dispenser of rights pertaining to it.

Here too, we may sum up the moral conception that prevails today in two points:

a) There is no universal moral law, whether religious or secular.

b) In the liberal (Western) world, the principle of *respect for the free value choices of individuals* reigns.

In this formula, both the points that were located at the beginning of our trajectory have vanished. From universality we have passed to relativity, and from the human person to the individual subject. Autonomy has become the new commandment, displacing the divine commandment and eliciting unanimous consent. Six liberal American philosophers turned to the Supreme Court of the United States as *amici curiae* in defense of two cases of suicide, claiming that "each individual has a right to make the most intimate and personal choices central to personal dignity and *autonomy*."[83] An Australian scholar of bioethics asserts: "In a liberal society, the only common morality or ethical consensus [is the] one founded on the primary liberal values—moral *autonomy*, autonomy-based equality and justice, and annexed values."[84] An English scholar affirms: "in the contemporary Western world human persons are characterized chiefly by their rationality, self-awareness, and desire for a degree of *autonomy* consistent with reasonable and (in the best dispensations) democratically adjusted requirements of responsible social living."[85] An Italian author maintains: "Questions of bioethics must be entrusted to the *moral autonomy* of those who personally experience them."[86] A *Manifesto of Secular Bioethics* published in Italy in 1996 proclaims: "The prime principle inspiring our secularity is *autonomy*." The *New Manifesto of Secular Bioethics* of 2007 states: "At the heart of existence there are a few key values, such as respect for *individual liberty and self-determination*." The whole West is united in this struggle for autonomy, as if there were no limit to it, not even that respect for the human person which is the very basis of liberal doctrine. Perhaps Mill would have been pleased, but he most certainly would have been disturbed to observe that his liberal struggle against the interference of the state has become a democratic request for the state to create rights by means of laws, thus interfering with autonomy, and thereby becoming illiberal.

Does religion put up a resistance to a state that decides what is morally good and bad? No worry, a "secular" solution is available. Since "religion is not only anti-moral, it is often immoral," therefore "the solution is to make the public domain wholly secular, leaving religion to the personal sphere, as a matter of private observance only."[87] Do ethical conflicts remain even when religion has been shut away in the private sphere? Another "secular" loophole is at hand: we must find "a reasonable balance [or ordering] of political values [on the issue] and citizens must simply vote on the question."[88]

Here we clearly see the crossroads or dilemma faced by liberal doctrine that I mentioned at the beginning of this book. Either liberalism embraces a given doctrine of the good, in particular that Christian doctrine which is its congener, and can offer something to address the contemporary moral crisis; or it keeps on claiming to be "self-sufficient" or "neutral" or "secular" or "only political," in which case it will remain extraneous to that crisis or even exacerbate it, to the detriment of us all. Contemporary liberalism chooses the latter road.

Note how the descending trajectory of liberal ethics and the corresponding one of the liberal state both departed from rigorous prohibitions and then plunged toward the most flexible permissions. The phases of this trajectory may be schematically summed up as follows:

1) It is prohibited to violate the moral commandments.
2) It is prohibited to violate the personal autonomy of the individual.
3) It is prohibited to set moral limits.

No philosophy of history determines that this downward trend of the trajectory is the necessary consequence of its point of departure. Rather, it is a deviation. To affirm that current liberal public ethics "is a result of a still-unbroken trust in scientific and technological development, particularly through the lens of the Lockean liberal tradition,"[89] is only half true. Blind faith in science is certainly a factor of deviation, but neither Locke nor the fathers of liberalism maintained ethical positions compatible with the current trend. They believed in God, in natural law, in the inalienable rights of man. Today that trajectory has reached its lowest point. Not only is God dead, but all comfort or assistance that religion might contribute to personal autonomy has vanished, and truly anything is allowed.

TO CONCLUDE: WHY WE SHOULD CALL OURSELVES CHRISTIANS

Can we reverse the direction of this trajectory? If we wish to avoid an even more serious moral crisis, then *we must,* and all our efforts should be concentrated on this new commitment.

The prevailing principle of autonomy is too fragile and vague to support coherent ethical imperatives. The specialized literature on the theme of bioethics clearly shows this. Starting from a given principle, we reach one conclusion in one case, but a completely different conclusion in a similar case, and sometimes no conclusion at all. One has the feeling that first the author states his own preference, followed by an *ad hoc* argument to justify it. For example, how can we come to justify abortion and euthanasia if we begin with the principle that life is sacred?[90] How can we justify abortion starting from the premise that "the fetus is a human being, a person from the moment of conception?"[91] How can we "distinguish the inviolability of human dignity . . . from the nondisposability of pre-personal human life?[92]

As the descending trajectory of liberal ethics has shown us, there are basically two main schools of thought: the ethics of principles and the ethics of consequences. Both raise problems of their own.

The ethics of principles requires that those principles not only be stated, but also be interpreted and applied. For example: how should we interpret the commandment "Thou shalt not kill?" We may say, "Do not suppress human life." But which human life, of what quality, and in what circumstances? The ethics of principles requires an instruction manual.

The ethics of consequences also faces problems. Mill spoke of the "permanent interests of man." But what interests did he mean? How can they be measured? Human beings have diverse interests which are in contrast with each other. How may they be combined, ordered, and arranged in a hierarchy? For example, does our interest in prolonging human life count more than our interest in leading a life worth living? Or does our personal interest in putting an end to our life in certain circumstances count more than our family's interest in prolonging it? In the case of the embryo or fetus, is there anyone else's interest that should count, aside from the mother or surrogate who is carrying the child in her womb? The ethics of consequences requires a means for measuring our interests.

The two ethics are incompatible, but each may warn the other of its corresponding risks. The ethics of consequences runs the risk of making case-by-case evaluations: whatever choice an individual makes, there will be an outcome with which to justify it. The ethics of consequences may become an ethics of flexibility. The ethics of principles runs the opposite risk, that of becoming deaf to circumstances, counterintuitive, even inhumane. Thus the ethics of principles may become an ethics of blind diktat.

In practice we try to find an appropriate synthesis, but this is almost impossible in principle. To put it in Kantian terms, the ethics of principles *always* views man as an end; the ethics of consequences, *sometimes* only as a means. For one, life is a value in itself; for the other, the value of life depends on what we do with it. For one, dignity depends on life; for the other, dignity depends on the quality of life. The middle way between these two roads—to consider man sometimes in one light and sometimes in the other—is the way chosen by our liberal states today. Our ethical legislation at times pursues one policy and sometimes the other. This means that it establishes *no* principles at all. But ethics without principles is like ethics without truth: it may be fatally confused with pleasure, usefulness, individual or group interest, and then degenerate into egoism, convenience, condescension. Ethics cannot be painless. It exists in order to restrain instincts and pleasures by setting limits to them.

For centuries, Christianity has established these limits. If man is created in God's image and God loves man and is loved by Him, offending one's own person or others is impermissible because this would offend God. The classical Christian liberalism of the fathers made this fixed point the pivot of free society, the source of universal, innate rights of all human beings whatever their skin color, condition of health, or phase of biological development. We should not lose this tradition; instead we should go back and start from there, from the Christian and liberal concept of the human person, without which our liberal societies cannot stand.

Is that enough? Problems of interpretation and application also beset the concept of the human person. In a prevalently Christian environment, with recognized Christian authorities, the imperative to "respect the human person" is sufficiently clear-cut and accessible to reasonable minds. In a secular world, it is not. Who is a human person? All biological lives from the moment of their conception? The lives of more highly evolved forms? Lives endowed with consciousness? Lives with a certain life expectancy? Lives possessing self-awareness? Even if we could solve these problems, more would arise. The point is that there are conflicts of value that cannot be solved without a loss of some kind. There is always a *moral choice* to be made. But how? On what basis? Using what sort of reason? Is there a practical reason, or is reason confined within the limits of logic, calculation, and empirical evidence? If it is not, how can we "broaden the concept of reason," as Benedict XVI has invited us to do?[93]

Amidst our uncertainty on all these issues, people turn today to the "experts" as they once did to fortune-tellers, our blind trust verging on credulity. They are the consultants, confessors, masters, guides, and apostles of humanity who have come to replace parents, priests, philosophers. This explosion of confidence in "experts" is often touted as the triumph of enlightened reason, but instead it has buried reason. Kant claimed that in order to live in an enlightened society, everyone must look out for himself and make his own decisions, because "If I have a book to have understanding in place of me, a spiritual adviser to have a conscience for me, a doctor to judge my diet for me, and so on, I need not make any efforts at all."[94] Today we are in precisely the situation of having someone decide for us on all important issues. Bioethics is entrusted to gynecologists as toothaches are to dentists.

In the end, we must choose. As the history of liberalism and modernity shows, the Christian choice to give oneself to God, or to act *velut si Deus daretur,* as if God existed, has yielded the best results. This choice still has great advantages also in the field of public ethics. If we live as Christians, we will be wiser and more aware of the dangers we face. We will not separate morality from truth. We will not confuse moral autonomy with any free choice. We will not treat individuals, whether the unborn or the dying, as things. We will not allow all desires to be transformed into rights. We will not confine reason within the boundaries of science. Nor will we feel alone in a society of strangers or oppressed by a state that appropriates us because we no longer know how to guide ourselves.

I have tried to prove here that we should be Christians if we want to save liberalism, and that Europe and the West should once again appreciate their Christian heritage and roots if they want to pursue their liberal freedoms. I have argued that liberal regimes are better than others. I conclude with a more general statement. Our moral norms, and with them our coexistence and our institutions—the very same ones that have passed down and preserved for us the civilization in which we are living, at times troubled and afflicted, at times satisfied and hopeful— would wither and die if they were to cut themselves off from Christianity.

To conclude, we should—we *must* call ourselves Christians.

NOTES

INTRODUCTION: WHEN OUR HOUSE CATCHES FIRE

1. Popper 1996, pp. 243–44.
2. Croce 1949a.
3. Hayek 1967, p. 155.
4. Heidegger 2003.
5. Tocqueville 2004, I.xvii.3, p. 358.
6. Jefferson 1984a, p. 289.
7. John Adams quoted in Hutson 2005, p. 191.
8. Rorty 1989, p. 45.
9. Ratzinger in Ratzinger and Pera 2006, p. 68.

CHAPTER ONE: LIBERALISM, THE SECULAR
EQUATION, AND THE QUESTION OF CHRISTIANITY

1.   To limit ourselves to contemporary literature, this is the second intuitive principle established by Ronald Dworkin. "Liberals insist on the sanctity of a certain set of familiar individual rights to liberty; these include rights to freedom of expression, freedom of religious or moral conviction, freedom from racial, ethnic, or gender discrimination, due process of law, and rights of political activity and participation." See Dworkin 1995, p. 196. See also Kymlicka 1995, p. 80: "the defining factor of liberalism is that it ascribes certain fundamental freedoms to each individual. In particular, it grants people a very wide freedom of choice in terms of how they lead their lives." Abundant literature exists concerning the historical origins of the notion of subjective natural rights. See Tierney 1997. On the contemporary expansion of that notion, see Glendon 1991.

2.   As Greg Forster rightly says, "Liberalism will not remain the governing philosophy of western nations if it cannot give a moral account of itself that will satisfy the overwhelming majority of people who believe, through various religions, that the universe is divinely ordered." See Forster 2005, p. 4.

3.   This, in my view, is the core of Leo Strauss's criticism of Isaiah Berlin's "empirical" rather than "absolutist" foundation for the principles of negative liberty (see Berlin 2002). Writes Strauss: "We are still waiting to hear why Berlin's principles are taken by him as sacred. If these principles are intrinsically valid, eternally valid, one could indeed say that it is a secondary question whether they will or will not be recognized as valid in the future and that if future generations despise the eternal verities of civilization, they will merely condemn themselves to barbarism. But can there be eternal principles on the basis of

'empiricism,' of the experience of men up to now? Does not the experience of the future have the same right to respect as the experience of the past and present?" Strauss 1989, p. 16.

4.   For a critical examination of antiliberal objections to liberalism, see Holmes 1993.

5.   For a critical examination of these criticisms, see Buchanan 1989.

6.   For an overview, see Ryan 1993. For the debate between liberals and communitarians, see Mulhall and Swift 1996, the essays in Avineri and de-Shalit 1992, and Sandel ed. 1984.

7.   In Europe, the present-day crisis of liberalism is the second in less than a century. For the first—the transformation of liberalism into juridical positivism—John Hallowell's criticism is still useful and penetrating. See Hallowell 1943.

8.   Robert Talisse is correct when he writes that "Both 'liberals' and 'conservatives' are liberal in the philosophical sense of the term. Debates in the United States between Democrats and Republicans are *not* debates about liberalism in the philosophical sense." See Talisse 2001, p. 18.

9.   Joseph H. H. Weiler has coined the fitting expression "Christophobia." See Weiler 2003.

10.   I have raised this point in Pera 2008.

11.   See the excellent study by Jenkins 2007.

12.   On religion in Europe and the reasons for its decline, see Davie 2000. The statistics are pitiful. According to the 2002 survey conducted by the Pew Research Center, when asked if religion played an important role in their lives, 59% of Americans said yes, whereas among Europeans, 33% in the UK, 27% in Italy, 21% in Germany, and 11% in France responded in the affirmative. In a 2007 survey, when asked if morality required religious faith, a minority in the U.S., 41%, said no, while in Europe a majority answered in the negative: 86% in Sweden,

83% in France, 71% in Spain and Italy. These percentages are the reverse of what we find in the major Islamic countries, and the situation does not seem to be improving.

13.   Rawls 1996, p. 10.

14.   Rawls 1985, p. 388.

15.   See Habermas's remarks in Habermas and Ratzinger 2006, pp. 24, 29.

16.   Rorty 1989, p. 45.

17.   Ackerman 1980, p. 103.

18.   According to Kent Greenawalt, "The government of a liberal society knows no religious truth and a crucial premise about a liberal society is that citizens of extremely diverse religious views can build principles of political order and social justice that do not depend on particular religious beliefs." See Greenawalt 1988, pp. 216–17. For criticism of such views, see Quinn 1995.

19.   Barry 1990 offers a convincing criticism of this principle. See also De Marneffe 1990.

20.   John Rawls writes that "since the political conception is shared by everyone while the reasonable doctrines are not, we must distinguish between a public basis of justification generally acceptable to citizens on fundamental political questions and the many nonpublic bases of justification belonging to the many comprehensive doctrines and acceptable only to those who affirm them." See Rawls 1996, p. xix.

21.   On this point, see, among others, Wenar 1995, Hampton 1989, and Scheffler 1994.

22.   See Rawls 1999, p. 152: "reasonable comprehensive doctrines, religious or nonreligious, may be introduced in public political discussion at any time, provided that, in due course, proper political reasons—and not reasons given solely by comprehensive doctrines—are presented that are sufficient

to support whatever the comprehensive doctrines introduced are said to support."

23.   See Habermas 2008, p. 134: "all coercively enforceable political decisions must be formulated and justifiable in a language that is equally intelligible to all citizens." See also p. 130: "Every citizen must know and accept that only secular reasons count beyond the institutional threshold separating the informal public square from parliaments, courts, ministries, and administration."

24.   See Greenawalt 1988, p. 217: "public discourse about political issues with those who do not share religious premises should be cast in other than religious terms."

25.   These formulas of common sense correspond to the more sophisticated principle of neutrality as viewed by Bruce Ackerman: "A power structure is illegitimate if it can be justified only through a conversation in which some person (or group) must assert that he is (or they are) the privileged moral authority. *Neutrality.* No reason is a good reason if it requires the power holder to assert: (a) that his conception of the good is better than that asserted by any of his fellow citizens or (b) that, regardless of his conception of the good, he is intrinsically superior to one or more of his fellow citizens." See Ackerman 1980, pp. 10–11.

26.   Pena-Ruiz 2003. Emphasis mine.

27.   Ibid.

28.   Stasi Commission Report, 1.2.1.

29.   In the guidelines provided to French school officials, the French minister of education, François Bayrou, wrote that "the nation is not only a collection of citizens pursuing individual rights. It is a community of destiny." In quoting this passage, Gerd Baumann remarked, not without irony, "France is something more than a country of human beings whose civil liberties are guaranteed. France is a religion." See Baumann

1999, chap. 4, table 4.1. The situation seems to be more complicated, however. In a speech given in the ethnically mixed Parisian suburb of La Courneuve on January 5, 2010, Eric Besson, the French minister of immigration, stated that "France is not a people, nor a language, nor a territory, nor a religion; it is a conglomeration of peoples who want to live together. There is no French-born, there is a blending [*métissage*] of France." See Hewitt 2010.

30.   This is a reference to the concept of "positive secularity" as presented in Sarkozy 2004 (p. 15) and later reiterated by the French president.

31.   Locke 1988b, §4, p. 269.

32.   See Kant 1991a, p. 54.

33.   Humboldt 1903, p. 111.

34.   Bacon 2005, I.3, p. 16.

35.   Locke 1988b, §4, p. 269. Emphasis added.

36.   I have examined the flaws in the doctrine separating the religious sphere from the scientific one in Pera 1998.

37.   Locke 2003, p. 220.

38.   Ibid., p. 246.

39.   Galileo 1989, p. 283. Emphasis mine. The problem was repeated and has continued to repeat itself. Pius XII claimed that "the Church prizes the value of human reason," but speaking of "those questions which even though they may pertain to positive science are more or less connected to the truths of Christian faith," he added that "if such hypotheses were to go directly or indirectly against revealed doctrine, they cannot be admitted in any way." Encyclical *Humani Generis*.

40.   On the history of European anticlericalism, see Chadwick 1975.

41.   See De Lubac 1995.

42.   For an overview from the French Revolution to our day, Burleigh 2005 and 2007 are indispensable. Concerning the contribution of Christianity to Western and world civilization, Stark's trilogy is fundamental: 2001, 2003, 2005.

43.   See the *Syllabus of Errors,* Apostolic Constitution decreed by Pope Pius IX on December 8, 1864, respectively §80, §39, §9.

44.   Tocqueville 2004, p. 14.

45.   See "Law of Nature" in Locke 1997, p. 270.

46.   Jefferson 1984a, p. 289.

47.   Kant 1991b, pp. 112–13. Tocqueville raised a similar question: "how is it possible that society should escape destruction if the moral tie is released? And what can be done with a people which is its own master if it be not submissive to Divinity?" See Tocqueville 2004, I.xvii.2, p. 357. This is a central question for any liberal. See Rawls 1996, p. xviii: "How is it possible that there may exist over time a stable and just society of free and equal citizens profoundly divided by reasonable though incompatible religious, philosophical, and moral doctrines?"

48.   See Pera 2010.

49.   Kant 1991b, p. 112. The reference to James Madison's *Federalist* No. 51 is immediately evident: "If men were angels, no government would be necessary." See Hamilton, Jay, Madison 1992, p. 266.

50.   Locke 1988b, §95, p. 330.

51.   Concerning the religious philosophy underlying the U.S. Declaration of Independence, the classic study by Carl L. Becker, first published in 1922 and reprinted many times, is still of great help. See Becker 1970.

52.   Kant 1991b, p. 99.

53.   Kant 1996b, 6:94, p. 129.

54.   Ibid., 6:100, p. 135.

55. Locke 1954, chap. I, p. 119.
56. Ibid., chap. VI, p. 189.
57. Kant 1996b, 6:93, p. 129. The American Founding Fathers had the same idea. See, for example, John Adams: "Religion and virtue are the only foundations, not only of republicanism and of all free government, but of social felicity under all governments and in all combinations of human society." Quoted in Hutson 2005, p. 191. For further reference, see Hutson 1998.
58. Locke 1954, chap. VI, p. 187.
59. Kant 1996b, 6:97, p. 132. Emphasis mine.
60. Ibid., 6:94, p. 130.
61. Ibid., 6:94–95, p. 130.
62. Ibid., 6:153, p. 177; and Kant 1996a, 5:129, p. 244.
63. Kant 1996c, 8:429, p. 614.
64. Kant 1991c, pp. 45–46.
65. Kant 1991b, p. 113.
66. Ibid., p. 117.
67. Ibid.
68. Ibid., p. 94.
69. Ibid., p. 117.
70. Kant 1996b, 6:94, p. 130.
71. Ibid., 6:96, p. 131.
72. Ibid., 6:98, p. 133.
73. Ibid., p. 134. It is known that for Kant, the various types of experience all have their own rational principles (or synthetic, a priori judgments), which are the conditions that render them possible. Science: scientific knowledge is possible if experience is subjected to categories. Morality: a moral action is possible if the maxim of the will can be held as a universal law. Law: a right action is possible if it allows the free will of each person to coexist with the freedom of everyone else according to a universal

law. To these principles we may add another, which, however, Kant did not formulate in these terms, concerning the ethical state: a liberal, virtuous community is possible if all its citizens are subjected to divine will.

74.   Ibid., 6:94, p. 130.

75.   Kant 1996a, 7:36, p. 262.

76.   Jefferson 1984d, p. 1125. See also this anecdote about Jefferson: while he was on his way to church, a passerby stopped and stared in amazement. Jefferson explained, "No nation has ever yet existed or been governed without religion. Nor can be. The Christian religion is the best religion that has been given to man and I as chief magistrate of this nation am bound to give it the sanction of my example. Good morning, sir." Quoted in Hutson 2005, p. 193. Jefferson's relationship to religion has always been subject to debate. Notable studies include Cousins 1958, and Kramnick and Moore 1996.

77.   Jefferson 1984b, pp. 1087–88. This was also the opinion of many of the Founding Fathers of America. For example, Adams: "[Christianity] is the religion of reason, equity and love; it is the religion of the head and of the heart." Or: "The Christian religion is above all the religions that ever prevailed or existed in ancient or modern times, the religion of wisdom, virtue, equity, and humanity." Quoted in Cousins 1958, pp. 104, 99. In a letter to Jefferson of June 28, 1813, Adams wrote that "the general principles upon which the Fathers created independence" are "the general principles of Christianity," and added that "these general principles of Christianity are as eternal and immutable as the existence and the attributes of God." See Adams 1959, vol. I, pp. 339–40.

78.   Locke 2002, p. 197 [272].

79.   Just to give one example drawn from Locke: "For what reason is there for the fulfillment of promises, what safeguard

of society, what common life of man with man, when equity and justice are one and the same as utility? What else indeed can human intercourse be than fraud, violence, hatred, robbery, murder, and such like, when every man not only may but must snatch from another by any and every means what the other is in his turn obliged to keep safe." See Locke 1954, chap. VIII, p. 213.

80.   Concerning the (Christian) virtues of liberalism, see Kloppenberg 1998 and Berkowitz 1999. The relationship between (Christian) virtues and liberalism may be deduced indirectly from John Stuart Mill, where he, while founding his liberalism on utilitarianism, expressed a conviction that seems scandalous to modern liberals: "Despotism is a legitimate mode of government in dealing with barbarians, provided the end be their improvement, and the means justified by actually effecting that end. Liberty, as a principle, has no application to any state of things anterior to the time when mankind have become capable of being improved by free and equal discussion." See Mill 1991, pp. 14–15. Freedom, we might say, requires civil virtues.

81.   I take "tradition" in Popper's sense and according to Kenneth Minogue's second meaning. See Popper 1963, chap. 4; and Minogue 1963, chap. 3, section 6.

82.   Encyclical *Centesimus Annus*, §46.

83.   Letter to Diognetus V.1.

84.   Letter to the Galatians 3:28.

85.   Croce 1949a, p. 47.

86.   Ibid., pp. 37–38.

87.   Ibid., p. 41.

88.   Ibid., p. 44.

89.   Letter to Maria Curtopassi of August 30, 1942. It continues as follows: "Don't you feel that in this terrible world war what is in conflict is a conception of life that is still Chris-

tian and another conception that hearkens back to the pre-Christian era, or even to the pre-Hellenic or pre-Oriental, to reattach itself to what came before civilization: the barbaric violence of the horde? *Portae Inferi non prevalebunt.* Let's hope not." See Croce and Curtopassi 2007, p. 55.

90.   See Croce 1939, pp. 229–30.

91.   See Croce 1949b, p. 235. Similar statements about Christianity are scattered throughout Croce's philosophical and historiographical writings, as Antonio di Mauro has shown in an admirable reconstruction of the subject. See di Mauro 2001. He calls our attention to a passage from *Philosophy of Practice,* 1909, in which Croce anticipated the title of his 1942 essay: "After polemics carried out by Kant, it is impossible for a serious philosopher not to be 'Kantian' in ethics, just as after Christianity it was impossible not to be Christian." See Croce 1996, pp. 275–76.

92.   Croce 1927, p. 4.

93.   Ibid.

94.   Croce 1931, p. 18.

95.   See Croce 1927, p. 8.

96.   Croce 1949a, p. 38.

97.   Ibid., p. 46.

98.   Ibid., p. 47.

99.   Ibid., p. 37.

100.   Ibid., p. 47.

101.   Croce 1996, p. 306.

102.   Ibid.

103.   Croce and Curtopassi 2007, p. 58.

104.   Having "contemplate[d] with sovereign reverence" the act that built "a wall of separation between Church & State," Jefferson added, "Adhering to this expression of the supreme will of the nation in behalf of the rights of conscience, I shall see

with sincere satisfaction the progress of those sentiments which tend to restore to man all his natural rights, convinced he has no natural right in opposition to his social duties." See Jefferson 1984c, p. 510.

105. I agree with the principle set forth by Nicholas Wolterstorff: "Let citizens use whatever reasons they find appropriate, including then, religious reasons." See Wolterstorff 1997, p. 112.

106. Kant 1996a, 5:125, p. 241; and Kant 1998, A829 and B857, p. 689.

107. On this question, see Pera 2005.

108. Kant 1996a, 5:130, p. 245.

CHAPTER TWO: EUROPE, CHRISTIANITY, AND THE QUESTION OF IDENTITY

1.   Montesquieu 2008, p. 227.
2.   Ibid.
3.   Ibid., Letter 24, p. 34.
4.   Ibid., Letter 96, p. 132.
5.   Ibid., Letter 73, p. 102.
6.   Ibid., Letter 99, p. 137.
7.   Ibid., Letter 91, p. 125.
8.   Ibid., Letter 21, p. 30.
9.   Ibid., Letter 99, p. 136.
10.   Leonard, 2005, p. 54.
11.   Haseler 2005, p. 86.
12.   Reid 2004, p. 227.
13.   Rifkin 2004.
14.   Booker and North 2003, pp. 4, 601–2.
15.   Siedentop 2000, p. 111.
16.   Ibid. p. 139.

17.   Thornton 2007.

18.   Bat Ye'or 2005.

19.   Laqueur 2007.

20.   Kagan 2003.

21.   Bawer 2006.

22.   Weigel 2005a, 2005b, 2006, and 2007.

23.   According to the Eurobarometer, May 2008, 48% of Europeans have a positive image of the Union; 53% think it is good to belong to it; 50% trust in it; 42% know how it functions; 92% declare that they feel attached to their own country and 49% to the Union.

24.   In my view, the most informed, detailed, and disenchanted history of the attempts at European unification may be found in Booker and North 2003. See also Moravcsik 1998. The history of the idea of European citizenship and its outcome is discussed cogently in Maas 2007.

25.   Renan 1992, p. 54.

26.   Schuman 1958. See also this statement in Schuman 1964, p. 78: "This togetherness cannot and should not remain an economic and technical undertaking. It must be given a soul."

27.   De Gasperi 1979, p. 185.

28.   Adenauer 2006, p. 301.

29.   Quoted in Booker and North 2003, p. 75.

30.   For a few of these objections, see Grimm 1995.

31.   See Siedentop 2000, chap. 2.

32.   Referring to the preamble to the Charter of Nice: "The peoples of Europe in creating an ever closer union among them . . . ," which was inspired by the preamble to the U.S. Constitution, Roger Scruton has rightly noted, "No one had ever asked the peoples of Europe whether they wanted an 'ever closer union' or what they understand the phrase to mean." See Scruton 2006, p. 169.

33. A French scholar who appreciates cosmopolitanism has noted that "the idea of the *jus cosmopoliticum* can begin to be embodied by the *jus commune europeum.*" See Ferry 2000, p. 177.

34. Certainly some of them were aware of this. During the labors of the first convention, the Belgian representative Roger Lallemand stated, "I believe we must affirm that the charter is *independent of the particular history of the European Union,* and does not imply any reference to a history, culture, religion, or specific philosophy of its own." See Lallemand 2000. Emphasis mine.

35. As Roger Scruton has noted, "The UN Charter of Human Rights and the European Convention of Human Rights belong to the species of utopian thinking that would prefer us to be born into a world without history, without prior attachments, without any of the flesh and blood passions which make government so necessary in the first place." See Scruton 2006, p. 23.

36. See Maas 2007, charter, 6.1. The Laeken Declaration on the Future of the European Union, December 15, 2001, stated that "The European Union's one boundary is democracy and human rights."

37. See Müller 2007. Concerning constitutional patriotism as a philosophy of European unification, see Fossum 2003a.

38. Ingram 1996, p. 2. Emphasis mine.

39. Habermas 1998a, p. 159.

40. Resta 2001, p. 182.

41. Habermas 2001, p. 100.

42. The context in which constitutional patriotism first developed is examined in Fulbrook 1999 and Müller 2000.

43. The controversy arose after Nolte published an article in the *Frankfurter Allgemeine Zeitung* on July 24, 1980. Related

texts have been collected and translated in Knowlton and Cates 1993.

44.   Habermas 1989, p. 227.

45.   Ibid.

46.   Habermas 1992.

47.   As is well known, Kant favored the idea of a federation but not a super-state. "Each nation, for the sake of its own security, can and ought to demand of the others that they should enter along with it into a constitution, similar to the civil one, within which the rights of each could be secured. This would mean establishing a *federation of peoples*. But a federation of this sort would not be the same thing as an international state." See Kant 1991b, p. 102.

48.   Concerning the "Kantian way" of European unification, see Ferry 2005, in particular Part III. The term "Kantian" in a pacifist, unwarlike sense is used polemically against Europe by Kagan 2003. On Euro-American relations, see also Cooper 2004, Part III.

49.   Habermas 1998a, p. 118.

50.   Speaking of constitutional patriotism, David Miller wrote, "Subscribing to [the principles of a constitution] marks you out as a liberal rather than a fascist or an anarchist, but it does not provide the kind of political identity that nationality provides. In particular, it does not explain why the boundaries of the political community should fall here rather than there; nor does it give you any sense of the historical identity of the community, the links that bind present-day politics to decisions made and actions performed in the past." Miller 1995, p. 163.

51.   This was precisely the title of one of De Gasperi's last speeches devoted to Europe. See De Gasperi 1979, pp. 199–204.

52.   As Margaret Canovan has noted, "Americans are not so because they willingly accept the constitution but because being

American is in their blood." See Canovan 2000, p. 425. David Gelernter may perhaps be exaggerating a bit, but not overly so, when he states that Americanism is a religion, "the fourth great Western religion." See Gelernter 2007.

53.   Habermas 2006b, p. 78.

54.   Anti-Americanism is part of the pro-Europe leftist ideology. Derrida and Habermas's manifesto (see Habermas 2006b) celebrates February 15, 2003 as the birthday of European consciousness in memory of the demonstrations held that day in European capitals against the war in Iraq. For others, that day occurred earlier, with "Schroeder's declaration of independence in the summer of 2002," when the German chancellor said no to the United States concerning that same war. See Haseler 2005, p. 52. European anti-Americanism after 9/11 is treated in Berman 2004, and O'Connor and Griffiths 2006.

55.   Habermas 1998a, p. 118. See also Kumm 2005, p. 321: "universal principles of justice may be textually fixed in the constitution. But they derive their power to shape identities in the present from the connection with the struggles of the past and the ambitions for the future. By being connected to the particular history, ambitions and current political practices of a particular community, thick constitutional patriotism reflects the specificity of a particular community." See also Fossum 2003b, p. 4: "Constitutional patriotism provides one set of answers or recommendations for how to reconcile universal values with context-specific ones, whilst also retaining sensitivity to difference and diversity." See also Ferry 2005, pp. 67–68: "a political culture common to all nations belonging to the Community, along with a shared historical memory, is the substantial element of a moral community that reinforces the legal community already developed in the Union in order to become a true political community."

56.   Habermas 1998a, p. 161.

57.   Müller 2005, p. 18. Maas is more cautious, and rightly so: "the common European identity putatively flowing from common EU citizenship might advance the mutual understanding and trust that enable democratic citizenship, transforming the EU into a multi-national or supranational political community in which feelings of common loyalty reflect a shared patriotism rather than a common national identity. *Or perhaps not.*" See Maas 2007, p. 96. Emphasis mine.

58.   Habermas and Ratzinger 2006, p. 27.

59.   Ibid., p. 21.

60.   Ibid., p. 28. Emphasis mine. See also Habermas 1994, p. 135: "The neutrality of the law vis-à-vis internal ethical differentiations stems from the fact that in complex societies the citizenry as a whole can no longer be held together by a substantive consensus on values but only by a consensus on the procedures for the legitimate enactment of laws and the legitimate exercise of power."

61.   Habermas and Ratzinger 2006, p. 24.

62.   Ibid., p. 27.

63.   Ibid., p. 24.

64.   Ibid., p. 28.

65.   Habermas 1996, p. 448. Emphasis mine.

66.   Habermas and Ratzinger 2006, p. 26.

67.   Ibid., p. 25.

68.   Habermas 1998a, p. 44. Here he stresses that "the content of the universal presuppositions of argumentation is by no means normative in the moral sense."

69.   Habermas and Ratzinger 2006, p. 26.

70.   Habermas 1996b proposes a "discourse-theoretic justification of basic rights" (p. 118) or a "logical genesis of rights" stemming from a "discourse principle that is initially

indifferent vis-à-vis morality and law" (p. 121). Habermas's theory is that "communicative freedom exists only between actors who, adopting a performative attitude, want to reach an understanding with one another about something and expect one another to take positions on reciprocally raised validity claims. . . . One has the possibility of taking a yes or no position to a criticizable validity claim only if the other is willing to justify the claim raised by her speech act, should this be necessary" (p. 119). In reality, something much more important is needed. The interlocutors must first recognize themselves as moral persons and then as linguistic persons. The transition from actor (a pragmatic-logical notion) to person (an ethical-juridical notion) is a non sequitur. We cannot derive substantive notions such as rights from linguistic notions such as the practice of argumentation or from procedural notions such as the rules of democracy. In his rejoinder to Richard J. Bernstein, Habermas writes that "a political system based on the rule of law is not self-contained, but also depends on 'a liberal political culture' and a population accustomed to freedom." See Habermas 1998b, p. 384. This seems to contradict any discourse-theoretic foundation of rights.

71.   Ratzinger and Galli della Loggia 2004.

72.   The real answer was given by the official authorities. The French president Jacques Chirac said that "France is a secular state and as such it is not in the habit of asking for insertions of a religious nature in constitutional texts." The president of the European Convention, Valéry Giscard d'Estaing, stated that "Europeans live in secular political systems where religion does not play an important role." On this question, see Weigel 2005b and De Mattei 2006.

73.   Habermas 2006a, pp. 150–51.

74.   I am referring to the objections against liberal genetics that are expressed in Habermas 2003.

75.   Habermas 2008, p. 131.

76.   On November 22, 2002, at the second European Convention, which drafted the text of the Constitutional Treaty, the French representative Hubert Haenel claimed that "the affirmation of European identity must not base itself only on the promotion of common values that are universal, but must rest on what is specific to Europe: its cultural, humanistic and religious heritage, and its linguistic and cultural diversity." See Haenel 2002. On Feburary 25, 2003, his French colleague Jacques Floch replied, first by observing that such a point of view reflected "a particularly Christian conception of the religious heritage of Europe," and then adding, "the religious element does not constitute an identifying element for the European Union and there is no reason to introduce it into the text of the Constitution. Moreover, it is a constant in European history that religions have been one of the often tragic elements of European division." See Floch 2003. On January 22, 2003, the Spanish representative Joseph Borrell Fontelles was even more explicit, saying, "a lot of our values have been forged against the Church or the churches. If we are to celebrate historical heritage we should remember the whole story: with its religious wars; the massacres of the Crusades; the night of Saint Bartholomew and the Inquisition's autos-da-fé; Galileo and the forced evangelisations; pogroms and the turning of a blind eye to fascism." See Borrell Fontelles 2003.

77.   See De Lubac 1995.

78.   After years of silence, antireligious literature is increasing and has several champions and proponents. For the most sanguine positions, see Dawkins 2006, Dennet 2006, Harris 2004 and 2006. Despite the vocabulary and style employed and the

evidence provided, these theories are no more modern than the
positivist ones of the nineteenth century, or of old Lucretius:
tantum religio potuit suadere malorum ("to so much cruelty
religion could lead us"). Some claim that "God almost certainly
does not exist" and that "religion is a by-product of something else" (Dawkins 2006, pp. 158, 172). Others affirm that
"while religious people are not generally mad, their core beliefs
absolutely are" (Harris 2004, p. 72), and that "while believing
strongly, without evidence, is considered a mark of madness or
stupidity in any other area of our lives, faith in God still holds
immense prestige in our society" (Harris 2006, p. 67). The least
we can say about such statements is that their authors rely on
rather peculiar criteria of existence and evidence.

79.   The English philosopher John Gray comments: "America's peculiar religiosity is becoming ever more strikingly pronounced. It has by far the most powerful fundamentalist
movement of any advanced country. In no otherwise compara-
ble land do politicians regularly invoke the name of Jesus." See
Gray 2003, p. 23. In the eyes of secular Europeans, the issue of
prayer is particularly disturbing. Even Derrida and Habermas
considered it problematical. "In Europe a president who begins
his official functions every day with a public prayer and con-
nects his momentous political decisions with a divine mission is
difficult to imagine." See Habermas 2006b, p. 46.

80.   On the cultural differences (social and political) between
the European Union and the United States, see McCormick
2007, p. 137.

81.   Delanty 1995.

82.   See Fisher 1960, p. 16: "In Christianity, as sharply dis-
tinguished from Judaism, was a new test, a new principle of
organization for European society. To be a Christian was to
be admitted, as it were, into the fellowship of the European

nations. To be a non-Christian was to be an outcast and an enemy."

83.   See Benedict XVI 2006.

84.   Tocqueville 2004, II.i.3, p. 525. Twenty years earlier, Hegel had expressed a similar view: "it is fully fifteen hundred years since through the influence of Christianity the freedom of the person began to flourish, and at least in a small section of the human race takes rank as a universal principle." See Hegel 2008, §62n, p. 17.

85.   For this and other equivalent formulas, see Eco 1997 and Scola 2007.

86.   Scoditti 2001, chap. 9.

87.   Fisher 1995, p. 12.

88.   Haseler 2005, pp. 134–35.

89.   Reid 2004, p. 218.

90.   Leonard 2005, p. 25.

91.   Garton Ash 2005.

92.   De Weck 1999, p. 107.

93.   Zielonka 2006.

CHAPTER THREE: RELATIVISM, FUNDAMENTALISM, AND THE QUESTION OF MORALS

1.   On this issue, see Browne 2006.

2.   Minogue 2005, p. xii.

3.   Harman 1996, p. 4.

4.   Jefferson 1984a, p. 285.

5.   Ibid.

6.   Ibid., p. 287.

7.   Locke 1988b, §6, p. 271.

8.   Locke 1988a, §88, p. 206.

9.   Kant 1996d, II.8 (7:90–91), p. 306.

10. See Hegel 1975, p. 76: "For [Kant's] practical reason is the complete abstraction from all content of the will; to introduce a content is to establish a heteronomy of choice. But what is precisely of interest is to know what right and duty are. We ask for the content of the moral law, and this content alone concerns us." For Hegel's celebrated critique of Kant's categorical imperative, see Hegel 2008, §135n. Concerning Hegel's critique of liberalism, see Smith 1989 and Bellamy 2000.

11. See Hamann in Schmidt 1996, p. 155.

12. Ibid. In a letter to Jacobi in 1784, Hamann wrote: "For me the question is not so much What is reason? as What is language? It is here I suspect the basis of all paralogisms and antinomies can be found which are ascribed to reason: it comes from words being held to be concepts, and concepts to be the things themselves." See Schmidt 1996, p. 300.

13. See Herder in Berlin 2000, p. 223.

14. Nietzsche 1968, VIII 1, 7 (60), p. 481.

15. Derrida 1974, p. 158.

16. Feyerabend 1975, chap. 1.

17. See the first edition (1986) of Gray 1995.

18. Gray 1993, p. 284.

19. Gray 2000, p. 122.

20. Ibid., p. 109.

21. Ibid., p. 116.

22. Ibid., p. 135. See also p. 20: "nearly all ways of life have interests in common that make a modus vivendi desirable for them."

23. Ibid., p. 20.

24. Gray 1993, p. 288.

25. This is Richard Rorty's idea, according to which liberalism "can only be something relatively local and ethnocentric." See Rorty 1991, p. 176. Rawls is not a relativist, but a statement

he made has prompted Rorty to lead him down that road. See Rawls 1980, pp. 306–7: "What justifies a conception of justice is not its being true to an order antecedent to and given to us but its congruence with *our* deeper understanding of *ourselves* and *our* aspirations and *our* realization that, given *our* history and the tradition embedded in *our* public life, it is the most reasonable doctrine *for us*." Emphasis added.

26.   Parekh 2000, p. 110.

27.   Kymlicka 1995, p. 81.

28.   Ibid., p. 82.

29.   Ibid., p. 83.

30.   Popper 1963, p. 352.

31.   On this controversy, see Tamir 1999 on the priority of individual rights and Bauböck 1999 for the opposite view.

32.   Trevor Phillips 2005. A sharp journalist has collected the symptoms of the British situation in a very successful book. See Melanie Phillips 2006.

33.   Fortuyn 2001, chap. 1.

34.   In the United States, as is well known, the oath ends with the words "So help me God."

35.   Kant 1991b, p. 105.

36.   Ibid., p. 106.

37.   Ibid., p. 106.

38.   See Savage 2004 and Casanova 2006. See also Samuel P. Huntington's penetrating and partly prophetic analysis: "In Muslim eyes, Western secularism, irreligiosity, and hence immorality are worse evils than the Western Christianity that produced them." See Huntington 2002, p. 213. Jacques Ellul has called our attention to the opposite phenomenon: "Christians are attracted by an intransigent, infallible religion endowed with extreme logical rigor and exemplified by famous mystics. Christians are aware of the feebleness of common faith and the

general indifference to Christianity (though also aware that our society has a great need to believe, to give meaning to life, etc.)." See Ellul 2004, p. 47.

39.   See Ratzinger 2005, p. 33. See also p. 44: "The real antagonism typical of today's world is not that between diverse religious cultures; rather, it is the antagonism between the radical emancipation of man from God, from the roots of life, on the one hand, and the great religious cultures, on the other. If we come to experience a clash of cultures, this will not be due to a conflict between the great religions which of course have always been at odds with one another but, nevertheless, have ultimately always understood how to coexist with one another. The coming clash will be between this radical emancipation of man and the great historical cultures."

40.   On this point see Tinder 1989 and Lindberg 2007.

41.   Del Valle 2002, p. 41.

42.   Esposito 2002, pp. 119, 127.

43.   See Popper 1996, vol. 2, p. 238.

44.   Ellul 2004, p. 60.

45.   Benedict XVI 2006.

46.   Ibid.

47.   The quotations that follow are taken from Abd Allah bin Mahfuz bin Bayyah et al. 2006 and from Muhammadu Sa'ad Ababakar et al. 2007.

48.   Of the three possibilities, the first is the most probable, if we consider the definition of dialogue proposed by Prince Ghazi bin Muhammad bin Talal: "Dialogue is by definition between people of different views, not people of the same views. Dialogue is not about imposing one's views on the other side, nor deciding oneself what the other side is and is not capable of, nor even of what the other side believes. Dialogue starts with an open hand and an open heart. It proposes but does not set

an agenda unilaterally. It is about listening to the other side, as it speaks freely for itself, as well as about expressing one's own self. Its purpose is to see where there is common ground in order to meet there and thereby make the world better, more peaceful, more harmonious and more loving." See Ghazi bin Muhammad bin Talal 2007. Clearly this does not refer to dialogue in a technical sense. The dialogue to which the Jordanian prince refers is the act of speaking about oneself with another, a conversation, an exchange of information.

49.   Benedict XVI 2006.

50.   For a discussion of dialectic logic in scientific contexts, see Pera 1994.

51.   A serious scholar of Islam has written: "The secularized world is pleased by Islam's elimination of Christian elements . . . because it recognizes in this an element of its own agenda for secularization. In reality, Islam is seeking Islamization, not secularization. Islam rejects Christianity in order to replace it with Muslim law." See Samir 2008, p. 53.

52.   See Berlin 2002.

53.   In the many-colored rainbow of liberals, the *libertarians* are the most alarmed by this degeneration: "What should be clear by now is that most if not all of the moral degeneration and cultural rot—the signs of decivilization—all around us are the inescapable and unavoidable results of the welfare state and its core institutions." See Hoppe 2001, p. 197.

54.   Minogue rightly observes that "we should never doubt that nationalizing the moral life is the first step toward totalitarianism." See Minogue 2010, p. 3.

55.   Dawson 1998, p. 27.

56.   See Talmon 1960.

57.   See Bork 2003, p. 11. The term "imperialism" contains a devaluing connotation, but the fact to which it refers is also

admitted by those who appreciate it. See Dworkin 1993, p. 120: "Some of the most important political decisions that any community must make—decisions that in most other democracies have been or would be the subject of great political struggles—have been decided for Americans by judges rather than by elected representatives of the people."

58.   Melanie Phillips 2006, p. 68.

59.   Kant 1996e, AK 4:429, p. 80.

60.   Kant 1996a, AK 5:31, p. 164.

61.   Kant 1996f, AK 6:280, §28, p. 430.

62.   Ibid., AK 6:278, §26, p. 428.

63.   "Concubinage occurs when a person surrenders to the other merely to satisfy [sexual] inclination." See Kant 1997, AK 27:387, p. 158.

64.   Kant 1996f, AK 6:279, §26, p. 428.

65.   "The moral ground for so holding is that man is not his own property . . . one cannot make one's person a thing." See Kant 1997, AK 27:387, pp. 157–58.

66.   "The end of humanity in regard to this impulse is to preserve the species without forfeiture of the person." See Kant 1997, AK 27:391, p. 161.

67.   "Suicide is not permitted under any condition. Man has, in his own person, a thing inviolable; it is something holy that has been entrusted to us." See Kant 1997, AK 27:372, p. 147. Locke agreed with this for the same reason: "Though Man in that State of Nature have an uncontrollable Liberty, to dispose of his Person or Possessions, yet he has not Liberty to destroy himself, or so much as any Creature in his Possession. . . . For Men being all the Workmanship of one Omnipotent, and infinitely wise Maker . . . they are his Property. . . . And being furnished with like Faculties, sharing all in one Community of Nature, there cannot be supposed any such Subordination

among us, that may Authorize us to destroy one another, as if we were made for one another's uses, as the inferior ranks of Creatures are for ours." See Locke 1988b, §6, pp. 270–71.

68. Mill 1998, pp. 97–98.

69. Mill 1991, p. 15.

70. Ibid., p. 14.

71. Ibid., p. 16.

72. Ibid., p. 17.

73. Ibid., p. 102.

74. Ibid., p. 106.

75. Ibid., p. 109.

76. Ibid., p. 107.

77. Ibid., p. 115.

78. Ibid., p. 5.

79. Ibid., p. 15.

80. Ibid., p. 80.

81. Ibid., p. 81.

82. A typical example of the Millian mother is Judith Jarvis Thompson. A woman wakes up to find herself attached to the body of a famous violinist whose kidneys have been plugged into hers and who would die if he were unplugged. If the woman were told that the violinist's right to live prevails over her own right to choose, says Thompson, "I imagine you would regard this as outrageous." In her view, this holds as true for the fetus as for the violinist. See Thompson 1971, p. 49.

83. The petition was signed by Ronald Dworkin, Thomas Nagel, Robert Nozick, John Rawls, Thomas M. Scanlon, Judith Jarvis Thompson. See Dworkin et al. 1997, p. 47. Emphasis mine throughout the paragraph.

84. Charlesworth 1993, pp. 162–63.

85. Grayling 2004, p. 78.

86. Lecaldano 2005, p. 33.

87.   Grayling 2004, pp. 80, 236.

88.   Rawls 1996, p. liv n. 31, p. lii.

89.   Habermas 2003, p. 76.

90.   Dworkin tries to show how this may be done in 1993, chaps. 3 and 7.

91.   This is Thomson's thesis, 1992, p. 47.

92.   This is Habermas's position, 2003, p. 77.

93.   Benedict XVI 2006.

94.   Kant 1991a, p. 54.

BIBLIOGRAPHY

Abd Allah bin Mahfuz bin Bayyah et al. 2006. "Open Letter to His Holiness Pope Benedict XVI." Available at http://www. ammanmessage.com/media/openLetter/english.pdf.

Ackerman, Bruce. 1980. *Social Justice and the Liberal State.* New Haven, Conn.: Yale University Press.

Adams, John. 1959. *The Adams-Jefferson Letters: The Complete Correspondence between Thomas Jefferson and Abigail and John Adams.* 2 vols. Edited by Lester J. Cappon. Chapel Hill: University of North Carolina Press.

Adenauer, Konrad. 2006. *Testimonianza di amicizia.* In *De Gasperi: Storia, memoria, attualità,* edited by A. Ciabattoni and A. Tarullo. Soveria Mannelli: Rubbettino.

Avineri, Shlomo, and Avner de-Shalit, eds. 1992. *Communitarianism and Individualism.* Oxford: Oxford University Press.

Bacon, Francis. 2005. *The Advancement of Learning.* NuVision Publications.

Barry, Brian. 1990. "How Not to Defend Liberal Institutions." *British Journal of Political Science* 20:1, pp. 1–14.

Bat Ye'or. 2005. *Eurabia: The Euro-Arab Axis.* Madison, N.J.: Farleigh Dickinson University Press.

Bauböck, Rainer. 1999. "Liberal Justifications for Ethnic Group Rights." In *Multicultural Questions,* edited by Christian Joppke and Steven Lukes. Oxford: Oxford University Press.

Baumann, Gerd. 1999. *The Multicultural Riddle: Rethinking National, Ethnic, and Religious Identities.* London: Routledge.

Bawer, Bruce. 2006. *While Europe Slept: How Radical Islam Is Destroying the West from Within.* New York: Doubleday.

Becker, Carl L. 1970. *The Declaration of Independence: A Study in the History of Political Ideas.* New York: Random House.

Beiser, Frederick C. 1987. *The Fate of Reason: German Philosophy from Kant to Fichte.* Cambridge, Mass.: Harvard University Press.

Bellamy, Richard. 2000. *Rethinking Liberalism.* London: Pinter.

Benedict XVI (Joseph Ratzinger). 2006. "Faith, Reason and the University," Lecture at the University of Regensburg, September 12, 2006. At http://www.vatican.va/holy_father/benedict_xvi/speeches/2006/september/documents/hf_ben-xvi_spe_20060912_university-regensburg_en.html.

Berkowitz, Peter. 1999. *Virtue and the Making of Modern Liberalism.* Princeton, N.J.: Princeton University Press.

Berlin, Isaiah. 2000. *Three Critics of the Enlightenment: Vico, Hamann, Herder.* Princeton, N.J.: Princeton University Press.

————. 2002. "Two Concepts of Liberty." In *Liberty,* edited by Henry Hardy. Oxford: Oxford University Press.

Berman, Russell A. 2004. *Anti-Americanism in Europe: A Cultural Problem.* Stanford, Calif.: Hoover Institution Press.

Booker, Christopher, and Richard North. 2003. *The Great Deception: The Secret History of the European Union.* London: Continuum.

Bork, Robert H. 2003. *Coercing Virtue: The Worldwide Rule of Judges.* Washington, D.C.: AEI Press.

Borrell Fontelles, Joseph. 2003. Speech at the European Convention, Brussels, January 22, 2003. At http://european-convention.eu.int (Documents: Contributors: CONV 501/03).

Browne, Anthony. 2006. *The Retreat of Reason: Political Correctness and the Corruption of Public Debate in Modern Britain.* London: Civitas (Institute for the Study of Civil Society).

Buchanan, Allen E. 1989. "Assessing the Communitarian Critique of Liberalism." *Ethics* 99:4, pp. 852–82.

Burleigh, Michael. 2005. *Earthly Powers: Religion and Politics in Europe from the French Revolution to the Great War.* London: HarperCollins.

————. 2007. *Sacred Causes: The Clash of Religion and Politics, from the Great War to the War on Terror.* London: HarperCollins.

Canovan, Margaret. 2000. "Patriotism Is Not Enough." *British Journal of Political Science* 30:3, pp. 413–32.

Casanova, José. 2006. "Religion, European Secular Identities, and European Integration." In *Religion in an Expanding Europe,* edited by Timothy A. Byrnes and Peter J. Katzenstein. Cambridge: Cambridge University Press.

Chadwick, Owen. 1975. *The Secularization of the European Mind.* Cambridge: Cambridge University Press.

Charlesworth, Max. 1993. *Bioethics in a Liberal Society.* Cambridge: Cambridge University Press.

Cooper, Robert. 2004. *Breaking the Nations: Order and Chaos in the Twenty-First Century.* London: Atlantic Books.

Cousins, Norman. 1958. *"In God We Trust": The Religious Beliefs and Ideas of the American Founding Fathers.* New York: HarperCollins.

Croce, Benedetto. 1927. "Il presupposto filosofico della concezione liberale." In *Liberismo e liberalism,* by Benedetto Croce and Luigi Einaudi, edited by Giovanni Malagodi. Milan and Naples: Ricciardi, 1988.

———. 1931. "La religione della libertà." In *Liberismo e liberalism,* cit.

———. 1939. *Conversazioni critiche.* Serie quinta. Bari: Laterza.

———. 1949a, "Why We Cannot Help Calling Ourselves Christians." In *My Philosophy.* London: George Allen & Unwin.

———. 1949b. "Soliloquy of an Old Philosopher." In *My Philosophy,* cit.

———. 1996. *Filosofia della pratica.* Edizione nazionale. Naples: Bibliopolis.

——— and Maria Curtopassi. 2007. *Dialogo su Dio: Carteggio 1941–1952.* Milan: Archinto.

Davie, Grace. 2000. *Religion in Modern Europe: A Memory Mutates.* Oxford: Oxford University Press.

Dawkins, Richard. 2006. *The God Delusion.* Boston and New York: Houghton Mifflin.

Dawson, Christopher. 1998. *Christianity and European Culture: Selections from the Work of Christopher Dawson.* Edited by Gerald J. Russello. Washington, D.C.: Catholic University of America Press.

De Gasperi, Alcide. 1979. *De Gasperi e l'Europa.* Edited by Maria Romana De Gasperi. Brescia: Morcelliana.

Delanty, Gerard. 1995. *Inventing Europe: Idea, Identity, Reality*. London: Palgrave Macmillan.

De Lubac, Henri. 1995. *The Drama of Atheist Humanism*. San Francisco: Ignatius Press.

Del Valle, Alexandre. 2002. *Le Totalitarisme islamiste à l'assaut des démocraties*. Paris: Éditions des Syrtes.

De Marneffe, Peter. 1990. "Liberalism, Liberty, and Neutrality." *Philosophy and Public Affairs* 19:3, pp. 253–74.

De Mattei, Roberto. 2006. *De Europa: Tra radici cristiane e sogni post-moderni*. Florence: Le Lettere.

Dennet, Daniel C. 2006. *Breaking the Spell: Religion as a Natural Phenomenon*. New York: Viking.

Derrida, Jacques. 1974. *Of Grammatology*. Baltimore: Johns Hopkins University Press.

De Weck, Roger. 1999. "Neither Reich nor Nation: Another Future for the European Union." In *Reflections on European Identity*, edited by Thomas Jansen. Working Paper, European Commission Forward Studies Unit.

Di Mauro, Antonio. 2001. *Il problema religioso nel pensiero di Benedetto Croce*. Milan: Franco Angeli.

Dworkin, Ronald. 1993. *Life's Dominion: An Argument about Abortion and Euthanasia*. London: HarperCollins.

———. 1995. "Foundations of Liberal Equality." In *Equal Freedom: Selected Tanner Lectures on Human Values,* edited by Stephen Darwall. Chicago: University of Chicago Press.

——— et al. 1997. "Assisted Suicide: The Philosophers' Brief." *New York Review of Books* 5:44 (March 27, 1997).

Eco, Umberto. 1997. *Cinque scritti morali*. Milan: Bompiani.

Ellul, Jacques. 2004. *Islam et judéo-christianisme*. Paris: Presses Universitaires de France.

Engelhardt, H. Tristram, Jr. 1986. *The Foundations of Bioethics*. Oxford: Oxford University Press.

Esposito, John L. 2002. *What Everyone Needs to Know about Islam*. Oxford: Oxford University Press.

Ferry, Jean-Marc. 2000. *La question de l'état européen*. Paris: Gallimard.

———. 2005. *Europe, la voie kantienne: Essai sur l'identité postnationale*. Paris: Éditions du Cerf.

Feyerabend, Paul. 1975. *Against Method*. London: New Left Books.

Fisher, Herbert Albert Laurens. 1960. *A History of Europe*. The Fontana Library. London: Collins. (Orig. pub. 1935).

Floch, Jacques. 2003. Speech at the European Convention, Brussels, February 25, 2003. At http://european-convention. eu.int (Documents: Contributors: CONV 577/03).

Forster, Greg. 2005. *John Locke's Politics of Moral Consensus*. Cambridge: Cambridge University Press.

Fortuyn, Pim. 2001. *De islamisering van onze cultuur: Nederlandse identiteit als fundament*. Rotterdam: Karakter Uitgevers.

Fossum, John Erik. 2003a. "The European Union in Search of an Identity." *European Journal of Political Theory* 2:3, pp. 319–40.

———. 2003b. "The European Charter between Deep Diversity and Constitutional Patriotism." In *The Chartering of Europe: The Charter of Fundamental Rights and Its Constitutional Implications*, edited by E. O. Eriksen, J. E. Fossum, and A. J. Menéndez. Baden-Baden: Nomos.

Fulbrook, Mary. 1999. *German National Identity after the Holocaust*. Cambridge: Polity Press.

Galileo Galilei. 1989. "Letter to Castelli," December 21, 1613. In *The Galileo Affair: A Documentary History*, edited by Maurice Finocchiaro. Berkeley and Los Angeles: University of California Press.

Garton Ash, Timothy. 2005. *Free World: Why a Crisis of the West Reveals the Opportunity of Our Time.* London: Penguin.

Gelernter, David. 2007. *Americanism: The Fourth Great Western Religion.* New York: Doubleday.

Ghazi bin Muhammad bin Talal. 2007. *Response to Cardinal Bertone,* December 12, 2007. At http://www.acommonword. com/lib/downloads/Letter-to-Cardinal-Bertone-13-12-07. pdf.

Glendon, Mary Ann. 1991. *Rights Talk: The Impoverishment of Political Discourse.* New York: Free Press.

Gray, John. 1993. *Post-Liberalism: Studies in Political Thought.* London: Routledge.

———. 1995. *Liberalism.* Buckingham, UK: Open University Press.

———. 2000. *Two Faces of Liberalism.* Cambridge: Polity Press.

———. 2003. *Al Qaeda and What It Means to Be Modern.* London: Faber & Faber.

Grayling, A. C. 2004. *What Is Good? The Search for the Best Way to Live.* London: Phoenix.

Greenawalt, Kent. 1988. *Religious Convictions and Political Choice.* Oxford: Oxford University Press.

Grimm, Dieter. 1995. "Does Europe Need a Constitution?" *European Law Journal* 1:3, pp. 282–302.

Habermas, Jürgen. 1989. *The New Conservatism: Cultural Criticism and the Historians' Debate.* Translated and edited by Shierry Weber Nicholsen. Cambridge, Mass.: MIT Press.

———. 1992. "Yet Again: German Identity—A Unified Nation of Angry DM-Burghers." In *When the Wall Came Down: Reactions to German Unification,* edited by Harold James and Marla Stone. London: Routledge.

———. 1994. "Struggles for Recognition in the Democratic Constitutional State." In *Multiculturalism: Examining the Politics of Recognition,* edited by Amy Gutmann. Princeton, N.J.: Princeton University Press.

———. 1996. *Between Facts and Norms: Contributions to a Discourse Theory of Law and Democracy.* Cambridge, Mass.: MIT Press.

———. 1998a. *The Inclusion of the Other: Studies in Political Theory.* Cambridge, Mass.: MIT Press.

———. 1998b. "Reply to Symposium Participants, Benjamin N. Cardozo School of Law." In *Habermas on Law and Democracy: Critical Exchanges,* edited by Michel Rosenfeld and Andrew Arato. Berkeley and Los Angeles: University of California Press.

———. 2001. *The Postnational Constellation: Political Essays.* Cambridge: Polity Press.

———. 2003. *The Future of Human Nature.* Cambridge: Polity Press.

———. 2006a. *Time of Transitions.* Cambridge: Polity Press.

———. 2006b. *The Divided West.* Cambridge: Polity Press.

———. 2008. *Between Naturalism and Religion.* Cambridge: Polity Press.

——— and Joseph Ratzinger. 2006. *The Dialectics of Secularization: On Reason and Religion.* San Francisco: Ignatius Press.

Haenel, Hubert. 2002. Speech at the European Convention, Brussels, November 25, 2002. At http://european-convention.eu.int (Documents: Contributors: CONV 429/02).

Hallowell, John H. 1943. *The Decline of Liberalism as an Ideology.* London: Kegan Paul, Trench, Trubner & Co.

Hamilton, Alexander, John Jay, and James Madison. 1992. *The Federalist.* London: J. M. Dent.

Hampton, Jean. 1989. "Should Political Philosophy Be Done without Metaphysics?" *Ethics* 99:4, pp. 791–814.

Harman, Gilbert. 1996. "Moral Relativism." In *Moral Relativism and Moral Objectivity*, edited by Gilbert Harman and Judith Jarvis Thomson. Oxford: Blackwell.

Harris, Sam. 2004. *The End of Faith: Religion, Terror, and the Future of Reason.* New York: W. W. Norton.

———. 2006. *Letter to a Christian Nation.* New York: Alfred A. Knopf.

Haseler, Stephen. 2005. *Super-State: The New Europe and Its Challenge to America.* London: I. B. Tauris.

Hayek, Friedrich A. von. 1967. "Opening Address to a Conference at Mont Pélérin," 1947. In *Studies in Philosophy, Politics and Economics.* London: Routledge & Kegan Paul.

Hegel, Georg Wilhelm Friedrich. 1975. *Natural Law.* Translated by T. M. Knox. Philadelphia: University of Pennsylvania Press.

———. 2008. *Philosophy of Right.* Translated by S. W. Dyde. New York: Cosimo.

Heidegger, Martin. 2003. "Only a God Can Save Us." In *Philosophical and Political Writings.* New York: Continuum.

Hewitt, Gavin. 2010. "To be French." BBC News, January 6, 2010. At http://www.bbc.co.uk/blogs/thereporters/gavin-hewitt/2010/01/to_be_french.html.

Holmes, Stephen. 1993. *The Anatomy of Antiliberalism.* Cambridge, Mass.: Harvard University Press.

Hoppe, Hans-Hermann. 2001. *Democracy: The God That Failed.* New Brunswick, N.J.: Transaction Publishers.

Humboldt, Wilhelm von. 1903. "Ideen zu einem Versuch die Grenzen der Wirksamkeit des Staats zu bestimmen." In *Gesammelte Schriften,* vol. 1. Königlich Preussischen Akademie der Wissenschaften. Berlin: B. Behr's Verlag.

Huntington, Samuel P. 2002. *The Clash of Civilizations and the Remaking of World Order.* London: Simon & Schuster.

Hutson, James H., ed. 1998. *Religion and the Founding of the American Republic.* Washington, D.C.: Library of Congress.

———, ed. 2005. *The Founders on Religion: A Book of Quotations.* Princeton, N.J.: Princeton University Press.

Ingram, Attracta. 1996. "Constitutional Patriotism." *Philosophy and Social Criticism* 22:6, pp. 1–18.

Jefferson, Thomas. 1984a. *Notes on the State of Virginia.* In *Writings,* edited by Merrill D. Peterson. New York: Library of America.

———. 1984b. "Letter to Moses Robinson," March 23, 1801. In *Writings,* cit., pp. 1087–88.

———. 1984c. "Letter to Messrs Nehemiah Dodge and Others, a Committee of the Danbury Association, in the State of Connecticut," January 1, 1802. In *Writings,* cit., p. 510.

———. 1984d. "Letter to Dr. Benjamin Rush, with a Syllabus," April 21, 1803. In *Writings,* cit., pp. 1122–26.

Jenkins, Philip. 2007. *God's Continent: Christianity, Islam, and Europe's Religious Crisis.* Oxford: Oxford University Press.

Kagan, Robert. 2003. *Of Paradise and Power: America and Europe in the New World Order.* New York: Vintage Books.

Kant, Immanuel. 1991a. "An Answer to the Question: 'What Is Enlightenment?'" In *Political Writings,* edited by H. S. Reiss. Cambridge: Cambridge University Press.

———. 1991b. *Perpetual Peace: A Philosophical Sketch.* In *Political Writings,* cit.

———. 1991c. "Idea for a Universal History with a Cosmopolitan Purpose." In *Political Writings,* cit.

———. 1996a. *Critique of Practical Reason.* In *Practical Philosophy,* edited by M. J. Gregor and A. W. Wood. Cambridge: Cambridge University Press.

————. 1996b. *Religion Within the Boundaries of Mere Reason.* In *Religion and Rational Theology,* edited by A. W. Wood and G. Di Giovanni. Cambridge: Cambridge University Press.

————. 1996c. "On a Supposed Right to Lie from Philanthropy." In *Practical Philosophy,* cit.

————. 1996d. *The Conflict of the Faculties.* In *Religion and Rational Theology,* cit.

————. 1996e. *Groundwork of the Metaphysics of Morals.* In *Practical Philosophy,* cit.

————. 1996f. *The Metaphysics of Morals.* In *Practical Philosophy,* cit.

————. 1997. *Lectures on Ethics.* Edited by Peter Heath and J. B. Schneewind. Cambridge: Cambridge University Press.

————. 1998. *Critique of Pure Reason.* Translated and edited by Paul Guyer and Allen W. Wood. Cambridge: Cambridge University Press.

Kloppenberg, James T. 1998. *The Virtues of Liberalism.* Oxford: Oxford University Press.

Knowlton, James, and Truett Cates, eds. 1993. *Forever in the Shadow of Hitler? Original Documents of the* Historikerstreit, *the Controversy Concerning the Singularity of the Holocaust.* Atlantic Highlands, N.J.: Humanities Press.

Koran, The. Translated by Marmaduke Pickthall. New York: Alfred A. Knopf, Everyman's Library, 1930/1992.

Kramnick, Isaac, and R. Laurence Moore. 1996. *The Godless Constitution: The Case against Religious Correctness.* New York: W. W. Norton.

Kumm, Mattias. 2005. "The Idea of Thick Constitutional Patriotism and Its Implications for the Role and Structure of European Legal History." *German Law Journal* 6:2, pp. 319–54.

Kymlicka, Will. 1995. *Multicultural Citizenship: A Liberal Theory of Minority Rights.* Oxford: Oxford University Press.

Lallemand, Roger. 2000. Speech at the European Convention, September 26, 2000, morning session.

Lambert, Frank. 2003. *The Founding Fathers and the Place of Religion in America.* Princeton, N.J.: Princeton University Press.

Laqueur, Walter. 2007. *The Last Days of Europe: Epitaph for an Old Continent.* New York: St. Martin's, Thomas Dunne Books.

Lecaldano, Eugenio. 2005. *Bioetica: Le scelte morali.* Rome and Bari: Laterza.

Leonard, Mark. 2005. *Why Europe Will Run the Twenty-First Century.* London: Fourth Estate.

Lindberg, Tod. 2007. *The Political Teachings of Jesus.* New York: HarperCollins.

Locke, John. 1954. *Essays on the Law of Nature.* Edited by W. von Leyden. Oxford: Clarendon Press.

———. 1988a. *The First Treatise of Government.* In *Two Treatises of Government,* edited by Peter Laslett. Cambridge: Cambridge University Press.

———. 1988b. *The Second Treatise of Government.* In *Two Treatises of Government,* cit.

———. 1997. *Political Essays.* Edited by Mark Goldie. Cambridge: Cambridge University Press.

———. 2002. *The Reasonableness of Christianity.* In *Writings on Religion,* edited by Victor Nuovo. Oxford: Clarendon Press.

———. 2003. *Two Treatises of Government and A Letter Concerning Toleration.* Edited by Ian Shapiro. New Haven, Conn.: Yale University Press.

Maas, Willem. 2007. *Creating European Citizens*. Lanham, Md.: Rowman & Littlefield.

MacIntyre, Alasdair. 1985. *After Virtue: A Study in Moral Theory*. London: Duckworth.

McCormick, John. 2007. *The European Superpower*. New York: Palgrave Macmillan.

Mill, John Stuart. 1991. *On Liberty and Other Essays*. Edited by John Gray. Oxford: Oxford University Press.

———. 1998. *Three Essays on Religion*. Amherst, N.Y.: Prometheus Books.

Miller, David. 1995. *On Nationality*. Oxford: Oxford University Press.

Minogue, Kenneth. 1963. *The Liberal Mind*. Indianapolis: Liberty Fund.

———. 2005. "Multiculturalism: A Dictatorship of Virtue." Introduction to *The Poverty of Multiculturalism* by Patrick West. London: Civitas (Institute for the Study of Civil Society).

———. 2010. *The Servile Mind*. New York: Encounter Books.

Montesquieu, Charles-Louis de Secondat de. 2008. *Persian Letters*. Translated by Margaret Mauldon. Oxford: Oxford World's Classics.

Moravcsik, Andrew. 1998. *The Choice of Europe: Social Purpose and State Power, from Messina to Maastricht*. Ithaca, N.Y.: Cornell University Press.

Muhammadu Sa'ad Ababakar et al. 2007. "An Open Letter and Call from Muslim Religious Leaders to His Holiness Pope Benedict XVI: A Common Word between Us and You." At http://www.acommonword.com/lib/downloads/CW-Total-Final-v-12g-Eng-9-10-07.pdf.

Mulhall, Stephen, and Adam Swift. 1996. *Liberals and Communitarians*. Oxford: Blackwell.

Müller, Jan-Werner. 2000. *Another Country: German Intellectuals, Unification, and National Identity.* New Haven, Conn.: Yale University Press.

———. 2005. "A 'Thick' Constitutional Patriotism for the EU? On Morality, Memory and Militancy." At http://www.princeton.edu/~jmueller/CP-ThickCPEurope-JWMueller.pdf.

———. 2007. *Constitutional Patriotism.* Princeton, N.J.: Princeton University Press.

Nietzsche, Friedrich. 1968. *The Will to Power.* Translated by Walter Kaufman and R. J. Hollingdale. New York: Viking.

O'Connor, Brendon, and Martin Griffiths. 2006. *The Rise of Anti-Americanism.* London: Routledge.

Parekh, Bhikhu. 2000. *Rethinking Multiculturalism: Cultural Diversity and Political Theory.* New York: Palgrave Macmillan.

Pena-Ruiz, Henry. 2003. *Qu'est-ce que la laïcité?* Paris: Gallimard.

Pera, Marcello. 1994. *The Discourses of Science.* Chicago: University of Chicago Press.

———. 1998. "The God of Theologians and the God of Astronomers: An Apology of Bellarmine." In *The Cambridge Companion to Galileo,* edited by Peter Machamer. Cambridge: Cambridge University Press.

———. 2005. "A Proposal That Should Be Accepted." Introduction to Ratzinger 2005.

———. 2008. "Europe without God and Europeans without Identity." In *Religion and the American Future,* edited by Christopher DeMuth and Yuval Levin. Washington, D.C.: American Enterprise Institute Press.

———. 2010. "Liberalism, the Loyalty Problem and the Gift of God." In *Cultures and Rationality,* edited by Caridad Velarde. Pamplona (forthcoming).

Phillips, Melanie. 2006. *Londonistan*. London: Gibson Square.

Phillips, Trevor. 2005. "After 7/7: Sleepwalking to Segregation." Speech to the Manchester Council for Community Relations, September 22, 2005. At http://www.humanities.manchester.ac.uk/socialchange/research/social-change/summer-workshops/documents/sleepwalking.pdf.

Plato. *Republic*. In *The Collected Dialogues,* edited by Edith Hamilton and Huntington Cairns. Princeton, N.J.: Princeton University Press, 1963.

Popper, Karl. 1963. *Conjectures and Refutations*. London: Routledge & Kegan Paul.

———. 1996. *The Open Society and Its Enemies,* 2 vols. London: Routledge & Kegan Paul.

Quinn, Philip. 1995. "Political Liberalisms and Their Exclusions of the Religious." *Proceedings and Addresses of the American Philosophical Society* 69:2, pp. 35–56.

Ratzinger, Cardinal Joseph. 2005. *Christianity and the Crisis of Cultures*. San Francisco: Ignatius Press.

——— and Ernesto Galli della Loggia. 2004. *Storia, politica e religion*. Atti del Convegno del Centro di orientamento politico, Rome, October 25, 2004. *Quaderno 7*. Rome: CSM. At http://www.fondazione-rebecchini.it/old/Convegni/25Ott2004/25Ott2004.htm.

——— and Marcello Pera. 2006. *Without Roots: The West, Relativism, Christianity, Islam*. New York: Basic Books.

Rawls, John. 1980. "Kantian Constructivism in Moral Theory." In *Collected Papers*, edited by Samuel Freeman. Cambridge, Mass.: Harvard University Press, 1999.

———. 1985. "Justice as Fairness: Political not Metaphysical." In *Collected Papers,* cit.

———. 1996. *Political Liberalism*. New York: Columbia University Press (paperback edition).

———. 1999. *The Law of Peoples*. Cambridge, Mass.: Harvard University Press.

Reid, T. R. 2004. *The United States of Europe*. London: Penguin Books.

Renan, Ernest. 1992. *Qu'est-ce qu'une nation? Et autres essais politiques*. Paris: Presses-Pocket.

Resta, Eligio. 2001. "Demos, ethnos. Sulla identità dell'Europa." In *Una Costituzione senza Stato*, edited by Gabriella Bonacchi. Bologna: Il Mulino.

Rifkin, Jeremy. 2004. *The European Dream: How Europe's Vision of the Future Is Quietly Eclipsing the American Dream*. Cambridge: Polity Press.

Rorty, Richard. 1989. *Contingency, Irony, and Solidarity*. Cambridge: Cambridge University Press.

———. 1991. "The Priority of Democracy to Philosophy." In *Objectivity, Relativism, and Truth*. Cambridge: Cambridge University Press.

Ryan, Alan. 1993. "Liberalism." In *A Companion to Contemporary Political Philosophy*, edited by Robert E. Goodin and Philip Pettit. Oxford: Blackwell.

Samir, Khalil. 2008. *Islam: Dall'apostasia alla violenza*. Siena: Cantagalli.

Sandel, Michael, ed. 1984. *Liberalism and Its Critics*. Oxford: Oxford University Press.

Sarkozy, Nicolas. 2004. *La République, les religions, l'espérance*. Paris: Éditions du Cerf.

Savage, Timothy M. 2004. "Europe and Islam: Crescent Waxing, Cultures Clashing." *Washington Quarterly* 27:3 (Summer), pp. 25–50.

Scheffler, Samuel. 1994. "The Appeal of Political Liberalism." *Ethics* 105:1, pp. 4–22.

Schmidt, James, ed. 1996. *What Is Enlightenment? Eighteenth-Century Answers and Twentieth-Century Questions.* Berkeley and Los Angeles: University of California Press.

Schuman, Robert. 1958. Speech before the European Parliament, March 19, 1958.

———. 1964. *Pour l'Europe.* Paris: Nagel.

Scoditti, Enrico. 2001. *La costituzione senza popolo: Unione europea e nazioni.* Bari: Dedalo.

Scola, Cardinal Angelo. 2007. *Una nuova laicità: Temi per una società plural.* Venice: Marsilio.

Scruton, Roger. 2006. *A Political Philosophy.* London: Continuum.

Siedentop, Larry. 2000. *Democracy in Europe.* London: Penguin Books.

Smith, Steven B. 1989. *Hegel's Critique of Liberalism: Rights in Context.* Chicago: University of Chicago Press.

Stark, Rodney. 2001. *One True God: Historical Consequences of Monotheism.* Princeton, N.J.: Princeton University Press.

———. 2003. *For the Glory of God: How Monotheism Led to Reformations, Science, Witch-Hunts, and the End of Slavery.* Princeton, N.J.: Princeton University Press.

———. 2005. *The Victory of Reason: How Christianity Led to Freedom, Capitalism, and Western Success.* New York: Random House.

Stasi Commission Report. 2003. *Laïcité et République.* Paris: La Documentation française.

Strauss, Leo. 1989. *The Rebirth of Classical Political Rationalism: An Introduction to the Thought of Leo Strauss.* Edited by Thomas L. Pangle. Chicago: University of Chicago Press.

Talisse, Robert B. 2001. *On Rawls.* Belmont, Calif.: Wadsworth.

Talmon, Jacob Leib. 1960. *The Origins of Totalitarian Democracy.* New York: Praeger.

Tamir, Yael. 1999. "Against Collective Rights." In *Multicultural Questions,* edited by Christian Joppke and Steven Lukes. Oxford: Oxford University Press.

Thomson, Judith Jarvis. 1971. "A Defence of Abortion." *Philosophy and Public Affairs* 1:1, pp. 47–66.

Thornton, Bruce. 2007. *Decline and Fall: Europe's Slow-Motion Suicide.* New York: Encounter Books.

Tierney, Brian. 1997. *The Idea of Natural Rights: Studies on Natural Rights, Natural Law, and Church Law, 1150–1625.* Emory University Studies in Law and Religion. Grand Rapids, Mich.: Eerdmans.

Tinder, Glenn. 1989. *The Political Meaning of Christianity: An Interpretation.* Baton Rouge: Louisiana State University.

Tocqueville, Charles-Alexis Clérel de. 2004. *Democracy in America.* New York: Bantam Classic.

Weigel, George. 2005a. "Is Europe Dying? Notes on a Crisis of Civilizational Morale." American Enterprise Institute, New Atlantic Initiative, March–April 2005. At http://www.aei. org/outlook/22139.

———. 2005b. *The Cube and the Cathedral: Europe, America, and Politics without God.* New York: Basic Books.

———. 2006. "Europe's Two Culture Wars." *Commentary,* May. At http://www.commentarymagazine.com/article/ europe's-two-culture-wars/.

———. 2007. *Faith, Reason, and the War Against Jihadism: A Call to Action.* New York: Doubleday.

Weiler, Joseph H. H. 2003. *Un'Europa cristiana: Un saggio esplorativo.* Milan: BUR Saggi.

Wenar, Leif. 1995. "Political Liberalism: An Internal Critique." *Ethics* 106:1, pp. 32–62.

Wolterstorff, Nicholas. 1997. "The Role of Religion in Decision and Discussion of Political Issues." In *Religion in the Public Square: The Place of Religious Convictions in Political Debate,* by Robert Audi and Nicholas Wolterstorff. Lanham, Md.: Rowman & Littlefield.

Zielonka, Jan. 2006. *Europe as Empire: The Nature of the Enlarged European Union.* Oxford: Oxford University Press.

INDEX